Frantz Fanon

Revolutionary Lives

Series Editors: Sarah Irving, University of Edinburgh;
Professor Paul Le Blanc, La Roche College, Pittsburgh

Revolutionary Lives is a series of short, critical biographies of radical figures from throughout history. The books are sympathetic but not sycophantic, and the intention is to present a balanced and, where necessary, critical evaluation of the individual's place in their political field, putting their actions and achievements in context and exploring issues raised by their lives, such as the use or rejection of violence, nationalism, or gender in political activism. While individuals are the subject of the books, their personal lives are dealt with lightly except insofar as they mesh with political concerns. The focus is on the contribution these revolutionaries made to history, an examination of how far they achieved their aims in improving the lives of the oppressed and exploited, and how they can continue to be an inspiration for many today.

Also available:

Salvador Allende:
Revolutionary Democrat
Victor Figueroa Clark

Sylvia Pankhurst:
Suffragette, Socialist and Scourge of Empire
Katherine Connelly

Hugo Chávez:
Socialist for the Twenty-first Century
Mike Gonzalez

Percy Bysshe Shelley:
Poet and Revolutionary
Jacqueline Mulhallen

Leila Khaled:
Icon of Palestinian Liberation
Sarah Irving

Ellen Wilkinson:
From Red Suffragist to Government Minister
Paula Bartley

Jean Paul Marat:
Tribune of the French Revolution
Clifford D. Conner

Gerrard Winstanley:
The Digger's Life and Legacy
John Gurney

www.revolutionarylives.co.uk

Frantz Fanon

Philosopher of the Barricades

Peter Hudis

PlutoPress
www.plutobooks.com

First published 2015 by Pluto Press
345 Archway Road, London N6 5AA

www.plutobooks.com

Copyright © Peter Hudis 2015

The right of Peter Hudis to be identified as the author of this work
has been asserted by him in accordance with the Copyright, Designs
and Patents Act 1988.

British Library Cataloguing in Publication Data
A catalogue record for this book is available from the British Library

ISBN   978 0 7453 3630 5   Hardback
ISBN   978 0 7453 3625 1   Paperback
ISBN   978 1 7837 1684 5   PDF eBook
ISBN   978 1 7837 1686 9   Kindle eBook
ISBN   978 1 7837 1685 2   EPUB eBook

Typeset by Stanford DTP Services, Northampton, England
Text design by Melanie Patrick
Simultaneously printed by CPI Antony Rowe, Chippenham, UK
and Edwards Bros in the United States of America

Contents

Acknowledgements

I would like to thank Paul Le Blanc and David Castle of Pluto Press for their assistance and encouragement through all stages of creating this work.

Although my intellectual affinities and influences will be evident from the content of this book, no figure looms larger in shaping the ideas that gave birth to it than Raya Dunayevskaya (1910–87), who first alerted me to the power of Fanon's revolutionary humanism—and who, above all else, taught me how to *think*.

Introduction:
Fanon in Our Time

Fifty years after the formal end of European colonialism, and almost a decade after the United States had *seemed* to some to turn the corner on racism by electing its first black president, the specter of Frantz Fanon has returned—with a vengeance. Largely consigned to academic studies and debates over postcolonialism, difference and alterity for many years, Fanon's name suddenly went viral in December 2014. Within days of a New York City grand jury's decision not to indict the police officers who had strangled to death Eric Garner, an unarmed black man who was trying to sell a few cigarettes, a comment by Fanon appeared on numerous social media sites that was quickly picked up and quoted around the country—and in many parts of the world. It read: "When we revolt it's not for a particular culture. We revolt simply because, for many reasons, we can no longer breathe."[1] The statement seemed to capture the pain and poignancy of the moment, as tens of thousands of people poured into the streets—often spontaneously—to protest the injustice done to Garner as well as to Michael Brown, an 18-year-old black youth from Ferguson, Missouri who was murdered by a policeman that a grand jury likewise chose not to indict a few weeks earlier.

Actually, it turns out that the quotation from Fanon was somewhat truncated. The actual statement, made in *The Wretched of the Earth*, reads: "It is not because the Indo-Chinese discovered a culture of their own that they revolted. Quite simply this was because it became impossible to breathe, in more than one sense of the word."[2] Still, the fact that Fanon's words were quoted a bit out of context—a problem that has arisen repeatedly since his death in 1961—is less important than the fact that his ideas are seen by many to speak to the urgency of the moment. That the moment we are living through is urgent is clear—and most of all to blacks and Latinos in the U.S., as well as immigrants from Africa, Asia, and the Middle East facing heightened police abuse and racial and religious discrimination throughout Europe. Time seems to be marching backward in many respects, as xenophobic—as well as subtler but no less insidious—forms of racism seem to define the very shape of globalized capitalism in the twenty-first century.

Whatever was meant by the "promise," voiced following the collapse of statist communism in Eastern Europe and Russia in 1991, that a "new world order" was now before us based on principles of liberal democracy, it certainly has not brought us to a world any less "overdetermined" by racial profiling, racial prejudice, and racial injustice. Time seems to be marching backward indeed . . . but the question is, to what? To the kind of world that Fanon saw and criticized? To something even more barbaric? Or does the response by a new generation of activists and thinkers to what has aptly been termed "the new Jim Crow" in the United States foreshadow an effort to put all this aside, and reclaim what existing society repeatedly denies, especially to people of color—our *humanity*?

The challenges facing any effort to forge a revolutionary new beginning today are surely enormous. No sooner do new voices arise against the dehumanization that defines contemporary capitalism than they risk being subsumed by religious fundamentalist terrorism and the reactionary response to it by the Western powers. Violent attacks on journalists, feminists, Jews and others in the name of some mythical incarnation of "Islam," whether it occurs in France, Syria or anywhere else, testifies to how divorced today's apostles of mindless violence are from any liberatory impulse. The Islamic fundamentalists who murder civilians in France have the same aim as Christian fundamentalists who do the same in Norway or the U.S.—they wish to push history backward by provoking *permanent* inter-religious warfare (the same of course applies to Jewish fundamentalists in their attacks on Palestinians). No less mindless is the response of the Western powers—not only because of their persistent discrimination against immigrants, Muslims, and people of color but also because their response to religious-inspired terrorism is characterized by such a huge degree of *disassociation*. One would never know from listening to the pundits decrying the "clash of civilizations" that France murdered over a million Muslims in Algeria in the 1950s and early 1960s or that more recently the U.S. killed half a million in its misguided wars in Iraq and Afghanistan. Violence is always to be condemned—except when "we" engage in it, even when done on a massive and systematic scale and in complete disregard of human rights and international law. Today's voices of opposition are being continuously subsumed by state-sanctioned terror on one side and religious-misogynist terror on the other. Is there no way out of this cul-de-sac, which works so well for maintaining bourgeois social and ideological hegemony? Will it ever become possible to break through these mind-forged manacles by making the quest for a decent, living, *human* world a reality?

Whatever turns out to be the answer to this question, one thing is clear: Frantz Fanon was one of the foremost thinkers of the twentieth century because of his persistent effort to bring to the surface the quest for a new humanity in the social struggles of *his* time. Those struggles are long behind us now, and buried for the most part under a heap of disappointments and failures. So much is this the case that it is often hard to remember the promise of the anti-colonial movements of the 1950s and 1960s, how much they reordered world politics, and how many aspirations from common people they gave expression to. If for no other reason, Fanon's work is important in removing this layer of mnemonic debris left by over 50 years of aborted and unfinished revolutions.

We have more to recover, of course, than the past. It is the future that is most in jeopardy today, precisely because the effort to articulate the emergence of a new humanity from within the shell of old has so often fallen short. So can Fanon help reinvigorate the effort to develop a liberating alternative to the present moment? This is largely the question to which this study is directed. But we can only pursue it if we are first of all attentive to who Fanon was and where he was coming from in *his* moment.

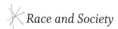

Race and Society

Fanon made it very clear, from the onset of his intellectual career, that "I'm not the bearer of absolute truths."[3] He resisted any pretense that the theoretician can hover over the world and give an objective accounting of it from afar. He understood, far better than most, that *each of us is the zero point of our orientation*. We can only know the world—and change it—from the vantage point of our situated experience. But the fact that I am the zero point of my orientation does not mean I cannot reach out to, and know, others. Nor does it mean that we cannot know absolute truths. He wrote, "As a man, I undertake to risk annihilation so that one or two truths can cast their essential light on the world."[4] One or two truths—that is all. It doesn't sound like much. But if those "one or two truths" turn out to connect us to our human potential that is now subsumed under an array of alienated forms and structures, would we not have made important progress in dealing with our present predicament?

The specter of Fanon *has* returned, and largely because he was one of the foremost thinkers of the last century on race, racism, and human liberation. It is precisely because we are not past the racism of the last century that we are not past Fanon: instead, we seem to be colliding into him, all over again. In doing so, what will we find?

One of Fanon's most important insights is that race and racism are not "natural" or biological factors but products of specific social relations. "Blackness" is neither a natural attribute nor a "fact."* "Blackness" is an objectified result of colonial domination—as is "whiteness." "It is the colonist who *fabricated* and *continues to fabricate* the colonized subject."[5] The formal end of colonialism by no means alters this, since "colonial racism is no different from other racisms."[6] *All* forms of racial classification and racism are a creation of historically conditioned social relations that have taken on a life of their own.

Fanon's insights hardly end here, however, since in stark contrast to today's social constructivists and postmodernists, he is not a determinist. He does not think we are the mere product and plaything

---

* The 1967 English translation of Fanon's *Black Skin, White Masks* by Charles L. Markman wrongly translated the title of chapter 5 as "The Fact of Blackness"—thereby ascribing to Fanon a view he did not hold. The original title in French—"L'expérience vécue du Noir"—is properly rendered as "The Lived Experience of the Black Man" in the more recent translation by Richard Philcox.

of ideological interpellation and social structures that are outside of our control. Instead, he grounds a negative critique of racism and dehumanization in a positive, affirmative vision of the human being who struggles to resist these conditions. He writes, "Man is a 'yes' resounding from cosmic harmonies."[7] *Contra* Martin Heidegger, Fanon insists, "Man is propelled *toward* the world and his kind."[8] We are not simply "thrown" *into* the world; we are *propelled* toward it and other *people*. We want "to touch the other, feel the other, discover each other."[9] *Our primordial ethical orientation is one of intersubjectivity.*

Racism radically distorts this orientation by locking individuals into their "whiteness" and "blackness." We become so habituated to being treated as racialized objects that we cease to *see* the other for who they *are*. As Lewis Gordon writes in his fine study of Fanon

Racism renders the individual anonymous even to himself . . . [it] either locks the individual into the mechanism of things or sends him away and transforms him into an observer hovering over that very thing. Thus, to be seen in a racist way is an ironic way of *not being seen* through *being seen*.[10]

This is the depravity and invisibility that Fanon spent his entire life critiquing and seeking to overcome. But he could not point the way to its overcoming unless he approached his subject matter from the standpoint of that which has not yet become fully objectified and reified—our human potential. We can only *see* beyond a certain limit if we already *stand*, in some sense, *beyond* it.

It is this stance that has receded from view in recent decades, as the tidal wave of structuralism, postmodernism, and postcolonial theory denies the possibility or validity of a humanist perspective. The result has been far from encouraging—an evisceration of revolutionary possibility and the loss of ability to envision a non-alienating future. This has an especially egregious impact when it comes to studies of Fanon, since it makes it all the more difficult to discern the *internal coherence* of his multifaceted work as a philosopher, political activist, psychiatrist, and revolutionary theorist. Many postcolonial theorists praise Fanon for issuing a virulent critique of the hypocrisy of European Enlightenment humanism, while expressing discomfort with his proclamation of "a New Humanism"[11] to replace it. Others emphasis his sensitive analyses of contingent realities and particular forms of oppression, while neglecting his effort to discern a pathway to "the universal"—understood by Fanon as "a world of reciprocal recognitions."[12] And others applaud Fanon for emphasizing local forms of subjugated knowledge in his analyses of Caribbean and African realities, while voicing irritation at him for elaborating what Henry Lewis Gates calls "a grand unified theory of oppression."[13]

To be sure, the problem of doing justice to the internal coherence of Fanon's thought has proved challenging for more than postcolonial theory. Adolfo Gilly presented Fanon (in his Introduction to *A Dying Colonialism*) as a veritable orthodox Marxist-Leninist, going so far as to write "For it is certainly obvious that, if in Algeria the masses had and have the inner life of their own that Fanon describes, the same life with the same aim exists in the Soviet Union, although it is expressed in a different form."[14] As if Fanon's sharp critique of the single-party state and his call to "leave this Europe . . . [which is] now teetering between atomic destruction and spiritual disintegration"[15] didn't imply a criticism of that totalitarian monstrosity! From the opposite perspective, the French social critic Alain Finkielkraut accused Fanon of advancing a variant of "European and *völkisch* nationalism" in his writings,[16] despite Fanon's sharp critique, not just of European nationalism but of nationalism itself in *The Wretched of the Earth* and other writings. And Hannah Arendt famously contended that Fanon's work is defined by the "metaphysics of violence,"[17] even though he did not write extensively on violence until his last book—which discussed violence in terms of the specific realities facing the Algerian and African independence movements of the 1950s and early 1960s instead of as a universal principle applicable to all situations.

One reason for the difficulty of accurately grasping what Fanon was about—and discerning the *unified* message that informs all of his work—is that his writings are easily misconstrued when abstracted from the philosophical framework that he is proceeding from. It is important to be attuned to that framework from the outset, even if its delineation must await the exploration of Fanon's life and work as a whole.

Fanon's Philosophical Standpoint

First, of foremost importance is the impact upon Fanon of phenom-enological philosophy. Phenomenology is a philosophical school of thought, first developed by Edmund Husserl at the beginning of the twentieth century, that focuses on being open to the immediacy of experience by bracketing out or suspending any attitude or claim about the world for which there is no *evidence* within our temporal and spatial horizon. The aim of the phenomenological method is to get us to "see" what the everyday, "natural" approach to the world conceals: our being-in-the-world as an active subject. By suspending any judgment about what is prior to or independent of our lived experience—such as what seems "natural" or "normal"—a path is opened to grasping the nature of things themselves, *including what it means to be human.*

Fanon became enamored of phenomenology early in his career, when he studied under one of the most astute continuators of Husserl's work, Maurice Merleau-Ponty, in Lyon, France in the late 1940s. Fanon's subsequent indebtedness to phenomenology is evident in virtually all of his work. He was especially taken with Merleau-Ponty's view in his *Phenomenology of Perception* that "no philosophy can afford to be ignorant of the problem of finitude."[18] Idealism and empiricism face great difficulties in adequately dealing with the finite character of our natural and social existence. Empiricism *reduces* mind to a *reflection* of finite objectivity, thereby presenting the world as given and immutable. This fails to account for how the human subject *shapes* the external world and reaches for "infinite" self-expansion.[19] Idealism envisions an active role for subjectivity but does so by reducing the world to the activity of an abstract constituting consciousness. In both cases our active inherence in *history* is obscured. In contrast, the phenomenological reduction aims to "bring back the living relationships of experience" by showing that "the world is not what I think, but what I live through."[20] This stress on the irreducible *interaction* between subject and object is one of the most important contributions of phenomenology.

Fanon makes direct use of this phenomenological approach in his critical analyses of colonialism and racism. He was especially attuned to Merleau-Ponty's insight that *the body* is our vantage point upon the world. Consciousness is never disembodied, as the idealists claim; nor does it merely exist in the form of an object, as the empiricists profess. In direct contrast to the mind-body dualism that pervades much of Western thought, phenomenology contends that consciousness is forever embodied, just as the *human* body is constantly "invaded" by consciousness. Merleau-Ponty held that when we ignore the vantage point provided by our "bodily-schema,"[21] social phenomena become treated as fixed, independent entities. The world is taken as a *given* and we appear as passive recipients of its messages. While such leading phenomenologists as Husserl and Merleau-Ponty did not delve into the issue of race, Fanon saw that their approach made it possible to philosophically comprehend "the lived experience of the black person." Colonial domination trains the eye to "see" skin color as an essential determinant of a person's being and character instead of as the social construct that it really is. This directly impacts the consciousness of both the victim and perpetrator of racism, by "fixating" them into certain roles and attitudes. As we will soon have occasion to see, all of Fanon's subsequent work—as philosopher, psychiatrist, and political activist—was aimed at liberating the human subject from the seemingly "innate" series of complexes that accompany this tendency toward fixation.

Second is the impact upon Fanon of Hegel's philosophy. This is evident in his first work, *Black Skin, White Masks*, which contains an explicit engagement with the "master/slave dialectic" in Hegel's *Phenomenology of Spirit*. What is often unappreciated, however, is the extent to which Hegelian ideas and concepts permeate Fanon's *entire* body of work—including his last book, *The Wretched of the Earth*. From his first moment of encounter with Hegel's philosophy, Fanon was especially attuned to its central category—the dialectical movement from the individual to the universal through the particular. Hegel summarizes this movement as follows: "Thus the object . . . is, as a totality, a syllogism or the movement of the universal through determination to individuality, as also the reverse movement from individuality through superseded individuality, or through [particular] determination, to the universal."[22]

From a phenomenological standpoint, the individual, the specific *person*, is not some abstract ego existing outside the world, but a being-for-itself saturated with the determinations of experience. The universal is that which all individuals aspire for—which Fanon defines as "a world of mutual recognitions" (that is, the "'I' that is 'We' and 'We' that is 'I'"[23]). The critical issue, in Hegelian philosophy, is that we move *from* the individual *to* the universal through the mediation of "specific determination"—the *particular*. Fanon will appropriate this notion by arguing that racial pride and national culture are not minor terms but rather *conduits to the universal* on the part of those facing colonial oppression and racial domination.

Third is the impact upon Fanon of the work of Karl Marx. Although Fanon was engaged in discussions and debates with Marxists from the beginning of his intellectual career, he never explicitly aligned himself with any specific current of twentieth-century Marxism—in large part, as we will soon see, because he did not think that they spoke to his lived experience as a black person. But this does not mean that Marxian *ideas* are not integral to his political and theoretical project.

Does this indicate that Fanon was a Marxist? The answer largely depends on what one means by "Marxism." If Marxism is defined as a series of fixed conclusions about social structures, the working class, and political organization that is applied to differing historical realities irrespective of their specific content, it is easy to contend that Fanon's heterodox views of the peasantry, the lumpenproletariat, and the centrality of anti-colonial struggles shows he was not a Marxist. Yet by the same token one could just as easily conclude that Marx was not a Marxist, given his insistence (voiced near the end of his life, and often against his own followers) that the non-Western world was not fated to repeat the course of capitalist industrialization delineated in Volume One of *Capital*—and that in Russia the *peasantry* was the major revolutionary force.[24] On the other hand, if "Marxism" is defined as a method of elucidating revolutionary possibilities from ever-shifting social realities, the situation appears quite different. Fanon stated in *The Wretched of the Earth*, "a Marxist analysis should always be slightly stretched when it comes to addressing the colonial issue."[25] *Slightly* stretched—but not rejected or abandoned. This *stretching* is evident from as early as *Black Skin, White Masks*, in which Fanon tackles an issue that was never discussed by Marx—the psychological impact of racism upon colonized peoples—while acknowledging that "the true disalienation of the black man implies a brutal awareness of social and economic realities."[26]

Fanon's emphasis on "disalienation" directly derives from Marx's theory of alienation. According to Marx, the fundamental problem of capitalism is not that it exploits workers by extracting more value from their laboring activity than they receive in the form of wages and benefits. The fundamental problem is much deeper—it is that workers become separated or alienated from their very *activity* of laboring in being treated as no more than a source of monetary value. In being alienated from our productive activity, we become alienated from our very humanity. Exploitation involves being robbed of the fruit of our labor, whereas *alienation involves being robbed of our very being.* Fanon views racism as the fullest expression of alienation, since blacks inhabit "a zone of nonbeing, an extraordinarily sterile and arid region, an incline stripped bare of every essential from which a genuine new departure can emerge."[27] Disalienation, the process of overcoming or transcending alienation, serves as the subject matter of all of Fanon's work—from his very first writings to his last. This study will have occasion to demonstrate this by exploring much of Fanon's relationship with Marx's thought.

These are by no means the only influences upon Fanon's life and work. His study of the major figures in European psychology—Freud, Adler, Reich, Jung, and Lacan—is of critical importance. After exploring the major figures of modern psychoanalytical theory in the 1940s, he went on to serve as a practicing psychiatrist for much of his adult life—a concern that he did not leave behind once he became an active revolutionary. Fanon did not attach himself to any of the leading schools of psychology, since their theories were developed irrespective of the actuality of racism and the lived experience of the colonized subject. As we will see, this did not prevent Fanon from making use of some of their major insights when it came to his effort to grapple with these issues.

No less important is the impact of such literary figures as Aimé Césaire and others who were part of the negritude movement. The impact of Césaire's political ideas and literary production upon the French West Indies cannot be exaggerated, and much of Fanon's work consisted of a dialogue with Césaire in particular—albeit one that became increasingly critical as he progressed in his intellectual career.

Most of all, Fanon was a student of life—of what he saw, heard, and experienced in *his* life, as lived first in the West Indies, then France, and finally in Algeria and Tunisia. Indeed, in exploring Fanon's work it is of utmost importance to be closely attentive to the specific situation and historical context in which he elaborates his ideas. One of the biggest mistakes made by both critics and followers of Fanon is to take his words out of context by detaching his pronouncements from the lived experience that produced them. Fanon addressed the world, but always from the zero point of his orientation. Does that voice still speak to us today? *Let us see.*

1

The Path to Political and Philosophical Commitment

Mountains of smoking ruins, heaps of mangled corpses, a steaming smoking sea of fire wherever you turn, mud and ashes—that is all that remains of the little city which perched on the rocky slope of the volcano like a fluttering swallow . . .

And now in the ruins of the annihilated city on Martinique a new guest arrives, unknown, never seen before—the human being. Not lords and bondsmen, not blacks and whites, not rich and poor, not plantation owners and wage slaves—human beings have appeared on the tiny shattered island, human beings who feel only the pain and see only the disaster, who only want to help and succor . . . A brotherhood of peoples against nature's burning hatred, a resurrection of humanism on the ruins of human culture. The price of recalling their humanity was high, but thundering Mount Pele had a voice to catch their ear.[1]

So wrote Rosa Luxemburg on May 15, 1902, of the massive volcanic eruption of Mount Pelée that a week earlier reduced to ashes the city of St. Pierre, in Martinique. Frantz Fanon probably never knew that this pivotal figure in European radicalism—who shared so many of his values, even if they differed on many others—had written so movingly of this event. Would he have been surprised to learn that a Polish-Jewish woman living thousands of miles away had the sensitivity to recognize that victims of the disaster came together to help each other in response to such a tragedy? Did the sense of mutual aid and brotherhood that arose from that event leave a trace, however indirectly, upon the social conscience of later generations of Martinicans, including Fanon's?

Before 1902 St. Pierre was the largest and most culturally developed city in Martinique, earning it the moniker "Athens of the Antilles." It went into rapid decline after the eruption of Mount Pelée (40,000 perished in all—a quarter of the island's population), and Fort-de-France soon replaced it as the center of Martinican urban life. It was to this city that Fanon's parents, Casimir Fanon and Eléanore Médélice, moved by the early 1920s, after growing up in a rural area on the Atlantic coast. And it was in Fort-de-France where Frantz, the fifth of their six children, was born on July 20, 1925. As it turned out, he would devote his life to what Luxemburg called "a resurrection of humanism on the ruins of human culture."

Growing up in Martinique

Martinique was a French colony (with intermittent periods of British rule) from the seventeenth century. Until the 1920s sugar cane was its leading export—thanks, initially, to the labor of African slaves. Slavery was abolished in 1848, but the subordinate position of blacks—the vast majority of the populace—continued largely unabated. Political and economic power remained in the hands of the *békés*—the descendants of white creoles, who numbered only 2,000 (out of a total population of 150,000) at the time of Fanon's birth. Nevertheless, despite the privileged position of the *békés*, Fanon did not grow up in a society defined by the rigid segregation and brutal racial oppression that existed in other colonies or the U.S. South. As he later wrote

> In Martinique it is rare to find hardened racial positions. The racial problem is covered over by economic discrimination and, in a given social class, it is above all productive of anecdotes. Relations are not modified by epidermal accentuations . . . In Martinique, when it is remarked that this or that person is in fact very black, this is said without contempt, without hatred. One must be accustomed to what is called the spirit of Martinique in order to grasp the meaning of what is said.[2]

This is reflected in the fact that until World War II blacks in Martinique did not refer to themselves as "Negroes." Nor did they tend to identify with their African roots. If anything, they were encouraged to disparage anything connected with Africa for the sake of emphasizing their presumed connection with France and French culture. Fanon did not grow up in a society in which racial self-definition—let alone "black pride"—was pronounced. In this sense, his experience very much coincided with that of Stuart Hall:

> When I was growing up in the 1940s and 1950s as a child in Kingston [Jamaica], I was surrounded by the signs, music and rhythms of this Africa of the diaspora, which only existed as a result of a long and discontinuous series of transformations. But, although almost everyone around me was some shade of brown or black (Africa "speaks"!), I never once heard a single person refer to themselves or to others as, in some way, or as having been at some time in the past, "African."[3]

Racism surely existed in Martinique, but at the time Fanon was growing up it was latent, taking the form of economic inequality and papered over by a large degree of self-denial. Gradations of skin color among those of African descent did not carry the same degree of social significance as found elsewhere. Fanon came from a middle-class family that generally had little everyday interaction with the *békés*, and his parents encouraged him to speak French instead of creole, the language of the "lower" classes, in his interaction with the larger society. It does not appear that experiencing overt racism from a very young age impelled him to eventually become a revolutionary.

So what *did* propel him to a life of political engagement? Why did he respond to his experienced conditions with a desire to ultimately change the world, while others who encountered the same or similar ones did not? This is a difficult question to answer about anyone, but it is made harder by the fact that Fanon rarely spoke about his past. He never gave an interview about his personal life and refrained from being drawn into discussing it when urged to by his friends. As he once told Marcel Manville, one of his best friends from Martinique, "One should not relate one's past, but stand as a testimony to it."[4]

What we do know is that when he was ten years old, in 1935, Fanon had a life-altering experience upon visiting the monument to Victor Schoelcher on a school trip. Schoelcher was a white Abolitionist who authored the decree of April 27, 1848 that abolished slavery in the French colonies. Fanon was suddenly struck by the thought of why was Schoelcher being honored while the slaves that he "freed" were not. He later told his colleague Alice Cherki

> It was the first time I saw that the history they were teaching us was based on a denial, that the order of things we were being presented with was a falsehood. I still played and took part in sports and went to the movies, but everything had changed. I felt as though my eyes and my ears had been opened.[5]

Perhaps this experience was one of those shocks of recognition from which a questioning and critical mind is born. It surely did not escape Fanon's attention that both the library he began visiting as a teenager (the Bibliotèque Schoelcher) and the school he attended (the Lycée Schoelcher) were named after this same figure— while the blacks who worked the sugar plantations under slavery, endured the "Black Codes," and suffered discrimination ever since remained invisible.

World War II: The Turning Point

The critical turning for Martinique and Fanon, both objectively and subjectively, was the year 1939. In October—shortly after the outbreak of World War II—a French military fleet commanded by Admiral Georges Robert arrived in Martinique. It was sent there by the French government to ensure that the fleet would not face a possible German attack. Along with the ships came 10,000 white French sailors—many of them virulent racists who took advantage of every opportunity to lord it over the native population. For the first time Fanon, like many others, had the opportunity to experience overt and systematic racist discrimination up close. After Germany defeated France in June 1940, Robert threw his lot in with the Marshall Philippe Pétain's collaborationist Vichy regime—an action that further exacerbated tensions with the black population, which largely identified with Republican France. Curiously, the U.S. recognized Robert's authority over the island in exchange for his agreement to keep the French ships under U.S. supervision; the U.S. still had formal diplomatic ties with Vichy France at the time, despite its collaboration with the Nazis (and it would continue to maintain them long after the U.S. actively entered the war).

Fanon later noted that in response to Robert's occupation "the West Indian underwent his first metaphysical experience"[6]—he began, for the first time, to see himself as *black*. The France to which many Martinicans had looked began to appear very different when it took the form of 10,000 white racist sailors abusing and demeaning them. As a result, the Martinicans began looking very differently at themselves. *A new sense of self emerged*. A *cultural* phenomenon—the formation of a black identity—was actually part of a *social* reflux, a response to the sudden influx of large numbers of white Europeans who vilified the Martinicans as "black." What Fanon later developed in his philosophical works— "It is the colonist who *fabricated* and *continues to fabricate* the colonized subject."[7]—was initially confirmed for him right here, in his lived experience following the arrival of the French fleet in 1939.

In that same year a critical subjective development occurred—the publication of Aimé Césaire's *Notebook of a Return to the Native Land*. Césaire, who by 1939 was also living in Fort-de-France and taught at the Lycée Schoelcher (which Fanon attended), broke new poetic, cultural, and political ground by not only declaring that Martinicans were black, but that they had every reason in the world to be proud of the fact. For Martinique, at least, this assertion of black pride marked something of an intellectual revolution—one that in time took the name of *negritude*. The colonial imposition of a black identity corresponded with an effort on the part of the colonized subject to invest it with liberatory content and significance. Fanon later wrote

[B]efore ten thousand racists, the West Indian felt obliged to defend himself. Without Césaire this would have been difficult for him. But Césaire was there, and people joined him in chanting the once-hated song to the effect that it is fine and good to be a Negro![8]

Negritude was still an emerging literary movement as of 1939. It was launched through the efforts of Césaire and other blacks from French-speaking colonies, such as Léon-Gontran Damas of Guiana and Léopold Sédar Senghor of Senegal. Influenced by the Harlem Renaissance as well as the literacy activity of blacks living in Paris in the 1930s, it became the foremost expression of self-assertion among French-speaking blacks in the years following World War II. For perhaps the first time in the Lesser Antilles, it proclaimed the need for a return to African sources and indigenous consciousness. In doing so, it sought to produce a social as well as psychological revolution among the victims of anti-black racism.[9] Although Fanon would develop a number of differences with the leading figures of negritude over the years, it would be no exaggeration to say that its two-fold concern with a social as well as psychological revolution was the humus from which his own distinctive approach to the critique of racism and colonialism would emerge. Fanon did not have to wait until the early 1950s, when he became a practicing psychiatrist, to become attuned to the psycho-affective dimension of race and racism. The idea was already in the air in the late 1930s, largely thanks to the poets of negritude.

In 1939, the 14-year-old Fanon was still too young to attend Césaire's courses at the Lycée. But he was already an avid reader, especially of literature and European philosophy. He appears to have developed a particular interest in Nietzsche as a teenager—an influence that will show up in much of his later published work. And he was taking in the work of Césaire, who began issuing the literary and artistic journal *Tropiques* in 1941 (eleven issues were to appear between then and 1945).

Fanon's Moment of Decision

The mid-1940s were not, for Fanon, a time for quiet intellectual reflection. The world was aflame in World War II and its impact reached even into such distant backwaters as the French West Indies. Increasing numbers of young Martinicans were leaving the island to join the Free French Army and fight the Nazis in Europe. In January 1943, Fanon—only 17 at the time—decided to do the same. He slipped out of Martinique during his brother's wedding and headed to the island of Dominica to meet up with other would-be resisters. Not long afterwards, a mass uprising—largely of urban workers—erupted in Martinique against Robert's administration. It marked the emergence (as Fanon later put it) of a new political consciousness—"the birth of the [Martinican] proletariat" as a revolutionary force.[10] Robert was forced out and Martinique's links to the Vichy regime were broken. Charles de Gaulle appointed Henri Tourtet as the new man in charge, and shortly afterward Tourtet organized a battalion of West Indians to fight with the Free French Army. Fanon enthusiastically returned to Martinique to join it.

Not all Martinicans were thrilled with the idea of joining De Gaulle's campaign to fight in Europe. Césaire denounced the whole idea on the grounds that blacks had nothing to gain by fighting in "a white man's war." Fanon thought differently. As one of his friends later recalled, he held that "whenever human dignity and freedom are at stake, it involves us, whether we be black, white or yellow. And whenever these are threatened in any corner of the earth, I will fight them to the end."[11] The sentiment is typically Fanonian. Less than a decade later, in his first published book, he emphasized the same concept by way of citing Karl Jaspers:

> There exists a solidarity among men as human beings that makes each co-responsible for every wrong and every injustice in the world, especially for crimes committed in his presence or with his knowledge. If I fail to do whatever I can to prevent them, I too am guilty.[12]

After undergoing basic training, Fanon was shipped off to North Africa in March 1944. All of those on board were black, except the commanding officers—who were white Frenchmen. Neither this nor the conditions he witnessed upon his arrival in Casablanca, Morocco escaped Fanon's attention. He was stunned to discover the extent of the strict racial hierarchy in the "Free" French Army. At the bottom were the Arabs, despised and discriminated against; then came the African troops (mainly from Senegal), segregated from other troops by distinct dress and in separate battalions; and then the West Indians, called "Europeans" by the French but under the command of white officers. Things were no better when the troops arrived in Algeria, where he saw at first hand the depth of hatred that many French settlers exhibited for native Jews and Muslims. Their animus had become even more accentuated during war, since many of the *pied noir* settlers enthusiastically embraced the racist and anti-Semitic laws adopted by the Vichy regime. This war for "human dignity" was beginning to wear somewhat thin.

Fanon nevertheless took part in the invasion of southern France in the fall of 1944. Sometime after the American forces secured the beaches, Fanon's battalion came ashore near St. Tropez. Fanon's unit later encountered heavy fighting further north, in the Doubs region near Montbéliard. In one of these battles he was seriously wounded by shrapnel, which landed him in the hospital for two months. For this he was given a Bronze Star—ironically, by the very man who would later lead French troops against the FLN in Algeria, Colonel Raoul Albin Louis Salan. Upon his release Fanon rejoined his unit and fought in the Battle of Alsace[13] in early 1945. But by this time he was thoroughly disgusted with the entire experience. He concludes that there is nothing honorable about fighting for the French. As he wrote to his brother Joby, "I've been deceived, and I am paying for my mistakes . . . I'm sick of it all."[14] Césaire was right; fighting for the French was not part of some "good cause."

The Postwar Years

After returning to Martinique in the fall of 1945, where he focused on completing his secondary education, Fanon studied under Césaire and became very close to him both intellectually and politically. In addition to absorbing his literary work and poetry, Fanon took part in Césaire's successful campaign to be elected to the French parliament as a member of the Communist Party. Fanon did not, however, share Césaire's enthusiasm for France's decision (in 1946) to transform Martinique from a colony to a département (*Département d'outre-mer*) of France. He also thought that the urbane Césaire did not have a good understanding of rural Martinicans.[15] Fanon's parents were originally from the countryside, and his interest in the peasantry shows itself rather early.

In this period Fanon reportedly engaged in some literary experiments, writing poems and drafts of several plays, but he made no effort to publish them and copies do not survive. Nevertheless, his literary voice was slowly beginning to take shape, directly influenced by the beauty of Césaire's verse and prose. No one who reads *Black Skin, White Masks*—as well as much of his later work—can avoid feeling the power and imagery of Fanon's writing, which has a poetic quality of its own. That voice, already taking shape while in Martinique, would in the coming years be enriched by his encounter with some of the major developments in European philosophy and literature.

Fanon was soon looking beyond Martinique. He was interested in pursuing a career and there was no university on the island. He toyed at first with the idea of becoming a lawyer, then a dentist. Taking advantage of a scholarship offered to war veterans, he decided to return to France. Paris was his destination—but not for long. He quickly grew bored of dentistry and decided to apply to medical school instead, in Lyon. It may not seem the most propitious location, given that Paris contained a large community of blacks from the West Indies whereas very few lived in Lyon. But this does not seem to have figured very large in Fanon's thinking. He even may have wanted to get away from the insular world of the Antillean community in Paris. In any case, by 1947 he was enrolled at the University of Lyon, taking courses in the medical school as well as in the philosophy department, where Merleau-Ponty was teaching.

Lyon may not have been the intellectual center that Paris was (and is), but in 1947 it was no backwater. Fanon had the chance to explore a number of intellectual currents at the university—from phenomenology and existentialism (which was then the rage in France) to Marxism and the psychoanalytical theories of Freud, Jung, and Lacan. He especially delved into the works of Jean-Paul Sartre, which influenced him greatly. Sartre's massive philosophic work *Being and Nothingness* had appeared in 1943, and its proclamation that humanity is "condemned" to create meaning and freedom in a meaningless world no longer sanctioned by the certainties of religion and belief in inevitable progress had an enormous impact. By 1947 it became impossible to escape the influence of Sartre and his circle (grouped around the journal *Les Tempes Modernes*). Fanon, like many others of his generation, dove deeply into Sartre's works. But what most caught his attention was his short book, *Anti-Semite and Jew* (written shortly after the liberation of France), which sought to explain the source of anti-Jewish racism.

In addition to attending courses by Merleau-Ponty and the anthropologist and art historian André Leroi-Gourhan, Fanon studied Kant, Kierkegaard, Jaspers, Levi-Strauss, and perhaps most important of all, Hegel. No less important, he was introduced to the works of the young Marx. The publication of the *Economic and Philosophical Manuscripts of 1844*, which was first published in the early 1930s after languishing in the archives for close to a century (and translated into French in 1935), was creating a huge stir at the time because of its discussion of alienation and humanism—not only among the Marxist but also Catholic and psychoanalytic left.

Lyon was a center of important discussions and debates in Marxist theory—both inside and outside the university. It had a sizeable industrial working class and virtually every tendency of the Marxist left—socialist, communist, Trotskyist—had a presence in the city. While some of Fanon's closest friends (such as Manville, now also living in France) followed Césaire into the Communist Party and Fanon was close to members of its youth branch, he never showed any interest in joining the party. It may be hard to appreciate today how rare that was in the late 1940s and 1950s. The French Communist Party (PCF) was *the* dominant political force on the left. In addition to being one of the largest political parties in France, is membership included, at one time or another, virtually every progressive intellectual in the country—from Foucault (a member from 1950–53) to Merleau-Ponty himself. Fanon was bucking the trend in not becoming swept into it. Even before arriving in Lyon, while still in Paris, he obtained and studied the works of Leon Trotsky as well as the proceedings of the Fourth International—something that was considered close to an act of treason (and at time punishable by physical assault) by those in and around the PCF. There are indications that Fanon may have had more contact with Trotskyists than many assume; it appears, for

Figure 1   Fanon in the 1950s

instance, that he crossed paths with Raya Dunayevskaya, Trotsky's former secretary who was later to found the philosophy of Marxist-humanism in the U.S., while attending a conference of socialist youth in Lyon in the summer of 1947.[16]

Fanon was also involved with the negritude movement, becoming part of the inner circle of its famous publication, *Présence africaine*, which was launched in 1947. He apparently also wrote for a literary journal addressed to students from the French colonies, *Tam-Tam*, though none of the pieces he authored for it have survived. He also became closely acquainted with the works of such U.S. authors as Richard Wright and Chester Himes through French translations of their works (Fanon's English would remain rudimentary for the rest of his life).

Fanon was also becoming more engaged in political activism, although he chose not to join any particular organization. He was involved in student politics at the university and participated in political demonstrations, some of them protesting colonialism. One biographer reports, "he was always involved in debates, going to left-wing meetings, touring occupied factories"—to the point that it was beginning to adversely affect his academic performance.[17]

Fanon had a lot on his plate, considering that he was engaged in these intellectual and political pursuits while attending to the rigors of medical school. But this was typical of Fanon. Throughout his adult life he slept only three to four hours a night and found time to explore many worlds at once. This included, not long after his arrival in Lyon, starting a relationship with Marie-Joséph Dublé, known as Josie, a French woman who at the time was studying liberal arts. They soon married and in the 1950s she bore a son, Olivier (Fanon also had a daughter, Mireille, from an earlier relationship with another French woman whom he did not marry). Josie Fanon was a theorist and political colleague in her own right. It was she to whom Fanon dictated much of the text of his first book, *Black Skin, White Masks* (he did not know how to type), and she later served as a staff member of the journal *Révolution africaine*.

The Shift to Psychiatry

Fanon's years in Lyon were clearly creative ones—not the least because he was formulating the ideas that became the subject matter of *Black Skin, White Masks*. Although published in the summer of 1952, he began working on what became its central theme in 1947 and by 1950 had formulated large portions of it.[18] Fanon was increasingly interested in the relationship between the social and psychological components of racism. He had already witnessed—at first hand in Martinique—how racial classification and identity is a construct of specific social relations. He had also studied enough social theory and Marxism to know that racism is closely bound up with economic conditions. But Fanon was hardly interested in stopping at that. Influenced by phenomenology and Sartre's existentialism, he wanted to make sense of the *interior* life of racism, its lived experience in terms of the actual individual. What kinds of neuroses are produced by racial discrimination—both on the part of its victim and perpetrator? What forms do they assume, and how universal are they? Most important, how can individuals experiencing alienation on account of racial discrimination become *disalienated* from the complexes associated with it?

These considerations, it appears, not only impacted Fanon's philosophical development but also his choice of a career. When in the fourth year of medical school, in 1951, he decided not to apply for a residency in medicine but instead to become a psychiatrist. Anxious to apply the insights he was gaining from his philosophical studies, a traditional medical practice now had less appeal to him.

Fanon completed his work in the psychiatry program under Professor Jean Dechaume and became a temporary intern at a hospital in Saint-Ylié in Dole, about 90 miles north of Lyon. When the time came for writing his thesis, he submitted an initial version of *Black Skin, White Masks*. Dechaume would have nothing of it on the grounds that it was permeated by "the author's subjectivity"[19] in a way that was unsuited for a scientific treatise. Facing intense opposition from his director, Fanon switched gears and quickly wrote a 75-page thesis dealing with the rather technical subject of Friedrich's ataxia (a hereditary degeneration of the spinal cord). Though a conventional piece of work, he made sure to preface it with a quotation from Nietzsche's *Thus Spoke Zarathustra*. Fanon apparently found it hard to suppress his rebellious side even at this point. But he defended the thesis successfully (in November 1951) and was now ready to do his residency in psychiatry.

Fanon at first accepted a position as a substitute physician at Colson in Martinique but soon returned to France, distressed at what he considered the impoverished state of psychiatry in the West Indies. He then took up a position at Saint-Alban, in central France. Fanon would work there for the next 15 months. It represented the first time he had the chance to directly apply the ideas he had been developing to a clinical environment. Saint-Alban would prove to be a critical experience in Fanon's life, as it was here that he learned about the principles of "socio-therapy" from its director, François Tosquelles, and gained hands-on experience in practicing it.

The Experience at Saint-Alban

Fanon's work as a psychiatrist will be explored in greater detail in chapter 3. Two points need to be singled out here.

First, Tosquelles's socio-therapeutic approach—which represented an effort not to control or repress the mentally ill but to listen to them and provide resources that could enable them to deal with their problems in a group environment—was developed as part of a *political* project. Tosquelles, originally from Catalonia, had been a militant in the Spanish Civil War of 1936–37 with the anti-Stalinist Marxists of the POUM (The Workers Party of Marxist Unification). After being forced to flee Spain for France, he became active in the French resistance against the Nazi occupation. While working in mental hospitals there he became painfully aware of the deleterious impact of their authoritarian and repressive practices. His participation in the resistance led him to introduce therapeutic approaches at Saint-Alban (where he became *chef de service* in 1952) that challenged what were then standard approaches in psychiatry. As David Macey notes, "The struggle against the concentration camp world of Nazism was continued by a struggle against the carceral world in which the insane were confined . . . [this] had brought Fanon to the heart of a psychiatric revolution that began with the Resistance."[20]

Many of the tools that Fanon would later use to combat the repressive nature of traditional forms of psychiatric treatment, both in France and later in North Africa, came from the lessons learned from a political struggle in the heart of Europe.

Fanon worked very closely with Tosquelles for the 15 months they were together in Saint-Alban—both as a practicing psychiatrist and in co-authoring three papers on psychiatry with him. They tried to humanize the institution by instituting communal living arrangements to end the isolation of patients and enable them to talk and relate to one another; give patients the freedom to roam around rather than being chained down in one spot; and circulating psychiatric reports to critical evaluation among the staff. The central principle was treating patients with dignity and viewing them as victims of alienation instead of as "innately deranged." Tosquelles expressed the approach thus: "Psychiatry cannot be reduced to a vision of man as just another variety of living organism. Psychiatry is a medical activity which must be based on a 'total' or 'anthropological' view of man including, at the same time, that which we would call the biological, the psychological, historic, and sociologic perspectives."[21]

Second, Fanon was attuned to Tosquelles's approach because he had already developed an understanding of many of these concepts before he even met him. As noted above, Fanon had been working as early as 1947 on a philosophical-psychological study that would become *Black Skin, White Masks*—long before he decided to embark on a career in psychiatry. In May 1951 he published a chapter of the book-to-be in *L'Esprit*, entitled "The Lived Experience of the Black Man." It contains some of the central themes that he is famous for—such as an investigation of the ramifications of the social construction of race and racism. *Alienation*—not just in its external social manifestation, but in terms of its inner psychic life within the individual—had become his major philosophical concern. No less central was *humanism*—an emphasis on the ability of the individual, if given the proper direction, to *disalienate* itself from the complexes associated with dehumanization.

The convergence between Fanon's philosophical and psychological investigations and Tosquelle's practice of socio-therapy is also shown by another one of his earliest published essays—"The North African Syndrome," published in February 1952. It begins by stating that we all must ask, "Have I not, because of what I have done or failed to do, contributed to an impoverishment of human reality?"[22] Fanon may have long before come to regret his decision to fight in World War II, but the *impulse* that led him to that decision is one that he never let go off. He furthermore writes

> Without a family, without love, without human relations, without communion with the group, the first encounter with himself will occur in a neurotic mode, in a pathological mode; he will feel himself emptied, without life, in a bodily struggle with death, a death on this side of death, a death in life . . . [23]

The "neurotic mode," according to Fanon, is a rupture from the communal—from our primordial relation to lived existence in which we "try to touch the other, feel the other, discover each other."[24] This is very much what Marx was getting at when he defined the ultimate form of alienation as the estrangement from humanity's species-being—from our capacity for conscious, purposeful activity as *communal* subjects.[25] What makes being alienated from the activity of laboring most egregious is that it leads us to become alienated from the creative dimension of our *being* as a species. When emptied of this human essence, our activity becomes monotonous and thing-like; as a result, the body ceases to be seen as inseparable from subjective *consciousness*. Instead, the bodily-schema becomes fixated, thingified, reified. Mind and body seem to inhabit different worlds. The fact that we are fixated insofar as we are viewed in terms of our bodies while our subjectivity escapes fixation is what makes the resulting neurosis so *painful*. As Hegel once put it, "It is said that contradiction cannot even be thought: but in the pain of the Living Entity it is even an actual existence."[26]

Fanon searched for a way out of this antinomy. He understood that "If YOU do not reclaim the man who is before you, how can I assume that you reclaim the man that is in you?"[27] The pathway to achieving this serves as the central theme of *Black Skin, White Masks*.

2

Self and Other: The Dialectic of Black Skin, White Masks

F anon's face-to-face encounter with the realities of racism, which assumed such a sharp and acute form from his experience of World War II and its aftermath, convinced him of the need to grasp the problem at its root. And grasping it at its root meant doing so *philosophically*. His study in Lyon had introduced him to a wealth of ideas that appealed to his effort to comprehend the actuality of his lived experience; phenomenology and existentialism, after all, emphasize action, immediacy, and engagement with the life-world as it presents itself to the living individual. However, by itself this could hardly satisfy Fanon's desire to come to grips with the actuality of race and racism, since most of the proponents of these schools of thought had shown little interest in such issues. Merleau-Ponty said virtually nothing about racism in his work (despite having written a famous book in 1947 devoted to politics, *Humanism and Terror*) and Fanon was unable to establish a rapport with him (Fanon found him to be cold and distant). Nor did the major figures in European psychoanalysis seem to have much to say about racism. Sartre, on the other hand, did produce an important essay in 1948 that addressed the dynamics of anti-black racism, "Black Orpheus" (which served as the introduction to one of the first collections of negritude poetry). But Sartre's discussion of race and racism (also developed in *Anti-Semite and Jew*) tended to be the exception rather than the rule among European philosophers.

At the same time, the negritude movement came into its own by the late 1940s. The search for a black identity and the need for a thoroughgoing critique of the racist basis of Western "civilization" were clearly in the air. While most European thinkers, including those on the left, tended to view the struggle against fascism and anti-black racism as being in separate compartments, Césaire openly proclaimed that the holocaust represented a series of genocidal acts against a European people that white Europeans had earlier imposed (albeit in a somewhat different form) against Africans and Native Americans.[1] The time was ripe for a philosophically grounded study of the impact of racism on the lived experience of black people, and Fanon saw it as his task to produce it. The result was *Black Skin, White Masks*, published in 1952.

Into the Depths of Racial Discrimination

Black Skin, White Masks takes us on a journey into a "veritable hell"[2] of fragmented and alienated human relations. We confront a world in which black people are "walled"[3] into their bodily-schema, treated as "an object among other objects,"[4] "stripped bare of any essential" to the point of inhabiting "a zone of nonbeing."[5] Their humanity rendered invisible by existing society, blacks fail to obtain the most basic recognition from whites—who likewise exist as an object among objects. We experience a world in which the victim and perpetrator of racism participates in a breakdown of intersubjective communion, a hollowing out of existence, a loss of individual subjectivity to the point where it seems

> . . . I was aware
> That I had strayed into a dark forest
> And the right path appeared not anywhere.[6]

To be sure, Fanon states at the start of the book, "our observations and conclusions are valid only for the French Antilles." Fanon always begins from the zero point of *his* orientation—that of a black man from the West Indies. Yet he soon adds "we shall enlarge the scope of our description to include every colonized subject." *All* colonized individuals, he declares, are "people in whom an inferiority complex has taken root."[7] The analysis and unraveling of this inferiority complex is his central concern.

Fanon is not interested, of course, in simply taking us deeper and deeper into this "veritable hell." Like Dante before him, "Our sole concern [is] to put an end to this vicious cycle." He aspires for a remedy to a world of distorted human relations in which blacks are locked into their blackness and whites into their whiteness. The title that he originally chose for the book expresses its liberatory intent: "An Essay on the Disalienation of the Blacks" (the title was changed to *Black Skin, White Masks* at the urging of his editor, Francis Jeanson). As he clearly states from the beginning, its defining perspective is "Striving for a New Humanism."[8]

But we must not move there too fast. Fanon often advises us to "move slowly"[9] as he presents his analysis. That is because we can only get to the positive—the overcoming of the affective disorders associated with discrimination and racism—by staring the negative in the face and *tarrying* with it. Rushing too fast over the negative will make it harder to comprehend the depth of the problem as well as trivialize the effort to overcome it. It is not that Fanon is holding something back on us. It's that he himself is unsure as to whether a "world of reciprocal recognitions" is really possible in societies structured by racism and colonialism. He *strove* and *reached* for a new humanism, but whether one can and will arise remained an open question for him, as it remains for us. It is the unfinished and unsettled character of the project that makes it so elusive, as well as compelling.

Fanon's Critical Encounter With Sartre

What proved of indispensable importance in Fanon's effort to tarry with the negative was the work of Jean-Paul Sartre. *Being and Nothingness* and *Anti-Semite and Jew* exerted a profound influence upon Fanon. Sartre argues in *Being and Nothingness* that humanity is not pre-determined by any fixed essence; instead, we become what we are through the *form* of interactions with others. This is never completely under our control, since we are "fixed" and defined by the "gaze" of the Other. We are constantly reaching to get in touch with our being, but that very being is defined by how the Other perceives and construes it. The form of our being is therefore never transparent. As he famously asserted, *nothingness resides in the very heart of our being*. I can get away from the gaze of the Other, which defines my being for me, no more than the Other can get away from my gaze that helps define his being.

Sartre's perspective was of great assistance to Fanon in formulating his conception that colonialism shapes the being of the colonized subject. Unlike the Jew, who (as Sartre discusses in *Anti-Semite and Jew*) is overdetermined by the view of themselves that they have interiorized from gentile society, blacks, Fanon contends, are "overdetermined from the outside"—that is, they are "slaves to their appearance."[10] Colonial domination, a rather arbitrary social construction, creates over time a certain way of "seeing," in which skin color is presumed to have determinative importance. The individual becomes fixated on the supposed "fact" of the person's blackness. This defines not only the colonizer's view of the colonized, but also the colonized view of themselves; they are "fixed" and defined by the "gaze" of the Other. Their "being" is defined by the Other—not by themselves. The black comes to see themselves as "black" because of the distorted gaze of the white—who is unaware, of course, that their way of "seeing" the Other is a result of the peculiar nature of colonial and racial domination. And since white society tends to associate "blackness" with every negative trait imaginable—again, as a result of its need to justify its domination over them—blacks come to view themselves as inferior to whites. For this reason Fanon writes, "The black man has no ontological resistance in the eyes of the white man."[11] Ontology refers to the nature of being—it is the study of what constitutes the real. Fanon contends that there is no ontology of blackness, since "blackness" is not a "natural" reality—it is not a form of being that just "is." Blackness is instead a construct of specific social relations. It is *produced*, *fabricated*, not simply *given*. The black "exists," as black, only in relation to the white: there is no pre-existing black essence that a black person can fall back upon. In other words, blacks "exist" and are defined in negative self-relation to what they are not.

Fanon therefore appropriates from Sartre his conception of the structure of human relations—*but only insofar as the issue of race and racism is concerned*. This qualification is of critical importance. Fanon denies that there is any ontology (or natural *fact*) of "blackness," since blackness, like all forms of racial identification, is a product of history. Sartre would no doubt agree. However, Fanon does not accept Sartre's characterization of human relations in general, *since that itself constitutes an ontology*—which, by definition, is independent of and prior to history. As Ato Sekyi-Otu put it in *Fanon's Dialectic of Experience*, "Sartre considers the danger of domination, alienation, and reification to be not a 'historical result' of an accident which is 'capable of being surmounted' but rather 'the permanent structure' of human interaction."[12] As Sartre himself put it, "We should hope in vain for a human 'we' in which the intersubjective totality would obtain consciousness of itself as a unified subjectivity."[13] For all of his critique of essentialism, Sartre embraces an ontological view of human existence in which "hell is other people." He denies the possibility, in principle, of the possibility of intersubjective communion. *This he does not see.*

Fanon, on the other hand, denies any such ontology since he proceeds from a phenomenological perspective—in which ontological claims are suspended and put aside. He does this to ensure that no hidden assumptions and biases predetermine what we "see"—such as a Hobbesian view of human nature in which hell is defined as other people. Fanon's insistence that "Ontology does not allow us to understand the being of the black man, since it ignores the lived experience"[14] is often taken as a critique of those who posit the existence of an undifferentiated "black essence"— and in many respects it is. But it also part of his effort to historicize what Sartre presents as the human condition. He does this because historicizing a situation or condition creates the possibility of seeing beyond it. As Karel Kosik aptly stated in *Dialectics of the Concrete*, "reality can be transformed in a revolutionary way only because, and only insofar as, we ourselves form reality, and know that reality is formed by us."[15] This is precisely the kind of transformation that Fanon is advancing toward: "There should be no attempt to fixate man, since it is his destiny to be unleashed. The density of History determines none of my acts. I am my own foundation. And it is by going beyond the historical and instrumental given that I initiate my cycle of freedom."[16]

Self and Other

But let us not move too fast . . . there is still much more to be said of the ramifications of being subjected to colonial and racial domination. It certainly involves economic and political discrimination. Fanon probes deeper, however, into its impact upon the inner psychic life of the individual. When you are judged as less than human because of the language you speak, the religious beliefs you uphold, or the color of your skin, there is a breakdown in the structure of mutual recognition. Your sense of self and dignity does not rest on you alone. It is formed and developed by being acknowledged and recognized by others. When that breaks down, you suffer from a weakened sense of self, a loss of self-esteem. The less recognition you receive, the more you want to get it; it is the lack that drives desire. The more this goes on, the more the Other becomes the focus of your thoughts and actions. You desire recognition so strongly that you become fixated on the Other—even as the Other continues to fixate you with its gaze into something you are not. It becomes a vicious cycle, in which appeals for recognition take on an increasingly desperate form. You appeal to the Other on the basis of *its* mores and values, hoping that by denying your attributes you will gain the recognition you deserve. You hate yourself for who you are in order to obtain the love that you aspire to receive. This is the inferiority complex that is so often associated with racial and ethnic discrimination. Fanon will demonstrate that it also shows itself in interpersonal relations between men and women. It can affect every aspect of your existence—how you dress, speak, behave, even think. The positive energy spent in focusing on the Other is in direct proportion to the negative energy spent in trying to escape from and deny your very self.

To tarry with this "veritable hell" it is necessary to move beyond a description of forms of discrimination and probe into the inner life of alienation. We must go deeper than the surface appearance, since alienation is never epiphenomenal. He writes, "We believe, in fact, that only a psychoanalytic interpretation of the black problem can reveal the affective disorders responsible for this network of complexes. We are aiming for a complete reversal of this morbid universe."[17]

Black Skin, White Masks develops this by making use of the insights of the major figures in European psychoanalysis. Although his knowledge of psychoanalysis was by no means exhaustive as of the writing of *Black Skin, White Masks*, Fanon draws from it a number of insights to aid his effort to come to grips with the subject of his analysis.

The psychoanalytic critique of fixation or morbidity is especially important for Fanon. Morbidity is a state of distress in which the subject becomes fixated. According to Freud, it is mainly a result of sexual trauma that has its roots in infantile sexuality. Subconsciously, the child is sexually attracted to the parent of the opposite sex while the parent of the same sex is seen as an object of competition that it wants to get rid of (the "Oedipus Complex" in boys and "Electra Complex" in girls). The subject's guilt over possessing these repressed desires is the source of most neuroses and psychic disorders. The subject of course tries to expel the memories of such childhood trauma from its consciousness, but it cannot rid itself of them; the repressed thoughts re-appear in another guise whose origin it is unaware of. This produces feeling of morbidity in the individual. Repression, while necessary, does not free us from neuroses, but rather makes them possible. The task of the analyst is to discover the *patterns* of neurotic behavior by finding their correlate in earlier familial relations.

Fanon does not question that many psychic disorders are associated with the contradictions of familial existence. He acknowledges that in European society "the family structure and the national structure are closely connected . . . There is no disproportion between family life and the life of the nation."[18] In both cases the *father figure* predominates. However, he adopts a critical stance towards Freud (as well as other figures in the psychoanalytical tradition, such as Lacan, Jung and Adler) on the grounds that their approach does not take account of the lived experience of the black person. He notes, "A normal black child, having grown up with a normal family, will become abnormal at the slightest contact with the white world."[19] It simply is not the case, he argues, that affective disorders that impact people of color can simply be traced back to relations within the family. They have a different source, which Freud's theoretical approach fails to account for. He writes

> Reacting against the constitutionalizing trend at the end of the nineteenth century, Freud demanded that that individual factor be taken into account in psychoanalysis. He replaced the phylogenetic theory by an ontogenetic approach. We shall see that the alienation of the black man is not an individual question. Alongside phylogeny and ontogeny, there is also sociogeny.[20]

Ontogeny refers to the developmental history of a person within their lifetime. In Freud, it points to the need to explore the aspects of an individual's experience that may contribute to neurosis or psychosis, such as family background, childhood experiences, etc. Phylogeny refers to the developmental history of a species. Whereas earlier thinkers viewed ontogeny as recapitulating phylogeny, Freud reverses this, insofar as our "natural" (phylogenic) development is largely dependent on a set of familial and childhood experiences (ontogenic) that impact the constitution of selfhood. Fanon follows Freud in this reversal, since he rejects any naturalist or biological understanding of what produces the affective disorders associated with racism. However, he takes issue with Freud for focusing exclusively on *individual* factors (like the parent–child relation) while ignoring the *social* determinants that impact the formation of selfhood. Freud may be able to explain disorders that pertain to some individuals, but he cannot explain those that pertain to people whose lives are shaped by racism. And he cannot do so because he ignores the role played by social relations (sociogeny) in the constitution of selfhood.

Fanon's vantage point upon the world is his situated experience. He is trying to understand the inner psychic life of racism, not provide an account of the structure of human existence as a whole. Racism is not, of course, an integral part of the human psyche; it is a social construct that has a psychic impact. Any effort to comprehend the social distress that accompanies racism by reference to some *a priori* structure—be it the Oedipal Complex or the Collective Unconscious—is doomed to failure.

Carl Jung sought to deepen and go beyond Freud's approach by arguing that the subconscious is grounded in a universal layer of the psyche—which he called "the collective unconscious." This refers to inherited patterns of thought that exist in all human minds, regardless of specific culture or upbringing, and which manifest themselves in dreams, fairy tales, and myths. Jung referred to these universal patterns as "archetypes." It may seem, on a superficial reading, that Fanon is drawing from Jung, since he discusses how white people tend to unconsciously assimilate views of blacks that are based on negative stereotypes. Even the most "progressive" white tends to think of blacks a certain way (such as "emotional," "physical," or "aggressive"), even as they disavow any racist animus on their part. However, Fanon denies that such collective delusions are part of a psychic structure; they are not permanent features of the mind. They are *habits* picked up and acquired from a series of social and cultural impositions. While they constitute a kind a collective unconscious on the part of many white people, they are not grounded in any universal "archetype." The unconscious prejudices of whites do not derive from genes or nature, nor do they derive from some form independent of culture or upbringing. Fanon contends that Jung "confuses habit with instinct."[21]

Fanon objects to Jung's "collective unconscious" for the same reason that he rejects the notion of a black ontology. His phenomenological approach brackets out ontological claims on both a social and psychological level *insofar as the examination of race and racism is concerned*. He writes, "Neither Freud nor Adler nor even the cosmic Jung took the black man into consideration in the course of his research."[22]

This does not mean that Fanon rejects their contributions *tout court*. He does not deny the existence of the unconscious. He only denies that the inferiority complex of blacks operates on an unconscious level. He does not reject the Oedipal Complex. He only denies that it explains (especially in the West Indies) the proclivity of the black "slave" to mimic the values of the white "master." And as seen from his positive remarks on Lacan's theory of the mirror stage, he does not reject the idea of psychic structure. He only denies that it can substitute for an historical understanding of the origin of neuroses.[23] Fanon adopts a socio-genetic approach to a study of the psyche because that is what is adequate for the object of his analysis.

For Fanon, it is the *relationship* between the socio-economic and psychological that is of critical import. He makes it clear, insofar as the subject matter of his study is concerned, that the socio-economic is *first* of all responsible for affective disorders: "First, economic. Then, internalization or rather epidermalization of this inferiority."[24] Fanon never misses an opportunity to remind us that racism owes its origin to specific economic relations of domination—such as slavery, colonialism, and the effort to coopt sections of the working class into serving the needs of capital. It is hard to mistake the Marxist influence here. It does not follow, however, that what comes first in the order of time has *conceptual* or *strategic* priority. The inferiority complex is originally born from economic subjugation, but it takes on a life of its own and expresses itself in terms that surpass the economic. *Both* sides of the problem—the socio-economic and psychological—must be combatted in *tandem*: "The black man must wage the struggle on two levels; whereas historically these levels are mutually dependent, any unilateral liberation is flawed, and the worst mistake would be to believe their mutual dependence automatic."[25]

On these grounds he argues that the problem of racism cannot be *solved* on a psychological level. It is not an "individual" problem; it is a *social* one. But neither can it be solved on a social level that ignores the psychological. It is small wonder that although his name never appears in the book, Fanon was enamored of the work of Wilhelm Reich.[26] This important Freudian-Marxist would no doubt feel affinity with Fanon's comment, "Genuine disalienation will have been achieved only when things, in the most materialist sense, have resumed their rightful place."[27]

The Inner Life of Racism

So what is the precise relation between the socio-economic and psychological, and how does Fanon delineate it? This is taken up in a chapter devoted to what may seem to have nothing to do with economics—"The Woman of Color and the White Man." It largely consists of a discussion of the novel *I am a Martinican,* by Mayotte

Capécia. Fanon does not think highly of the novel—he calls it "ridiculous" and "third rate."[28] His judgment may have been unfair; Capécia was the first black woman to be awarded the *Grand Prix Littéraire des Antilles* for the book.[29] In any case, he is interested in its portrayal of the main character—Mayotte, a black woman who is in love with a white man. Right away we see that something is amiss: "He is her lord." A "master/servant" relation is hardly a model of an authentic love relationship! She "loves" him because he is white; and what drives her to do so is her inferiority complex. How does this manifest itself? She is attracted to him because he has money and social status—which she lacks. A racial inferiority complex first shows itself in terms of an economic determinant. Fanon writes, "When we said in our introduction that inferiority had been historically felt as being economic, we were not mistaken."[30] And yet this is not where matters end, but only where they begin. "Her facticity was the starting point for her resentment."[31] She hates the fact that she "loves" him for his status and money, but she doesn't leave him. Her "love" of the Other is propelled by her resentment of the Other. This is not simply about economics; it isn't just a question of who pays the bills. It's a matter of a distorted form of intersubjectivity. She hates herself for being black, and by being with the Other she thinks she can become something she is not. But she cannot become that something else because she is black—*overdetermined* as such—and so she hates the Other for what she desires in him. Yet she hates herself even more and so the attraction to the Other continues unabated. A vicious cycle indeed!

Does this mean she is forever trapped? No, because "any criticism of being implies an answer."[32] Marx once wrote that humanity does not pose problems for itself that it cannot solve. Fanon thinks likewise. Alienation is not simply "given." It is not an *ontological* "fact." Nor is hatred a given. "It is a struggle to acquire hatred, which has to be dragged into being, clashing with acknowledged guilt complexes."[33] Since it is acquired, it can be unacquired. Mayotte wants to enter the white world because she has come to hate herself; her way out of that world, and into the human world, is to overcome her sense of self-hatred and inferiority. This is of course easier said than done. This is precisely *because* "Man is propelled toward the world and his kind."[34] The world that blacks are "propelled toward" is defined and structured by whites. The world has been defined *for* them, not *by* them. A retreat from the world is implausible, since blacks, like everyone else, are driven to actualize intersubjective communion with others. But no less implausible is the possibility of achieving communion with this white world. The subject feels trapped, with no way out—or in. "The inferiorized black man goes from humiliating insecurity to self-accusation and even despair . . . [his] attitude toward the white man or toward his fellow blacks often reproduces a delirious constellation that borders on the pathological."[35]

Fanon probes deeper into this pathology in the next chapter, "The Man of Color and the White Woman." Basing himself on the novel by René Maran, *Un home pareil aux autres*, Fanon explores the character of Jean Veneuse, a black man who tries to be white by forming a relation with a white woman. Like everyone else, he cannot live in a world without love, but it seems that the doors to love are blocked. He feels wounded, but the wound is *self*-inflicted. The reason is that he suffers from an abandonment neurosis. At one point in life, as a child, he "attempted an object relation . . . and was abandoned." He responds to the pain of the situation by wanting to make "the other suffer, and abandoning the other will be the direct expression of my need for revenge."[36] He runs away from the object of his affection because of his lack of self-esteem and finds himself unable to forge intimate ties with others. He is constantly ill at ease, and must repeatedly seek confirmation of his relationship in the assuring words of his partner. But the more he tries to convince himself of her love, the more obvious becomes the unhealthy nature of his relationship.

Fanon is going beyond discrimination and exploitation to the inner recesses of alienation. What makes alienation so painful is that it is *self*-inflicted. The wounds inflicted by the external world are never painful as those imposed upon oneself. Blacks are "enslaved" to their inferiority just as whites are "enslaved" to their superiority. Just when the door seems to slam shut on any resolution, however, Fanon reminds us "our aim is to enable healthy relations between blacks and whites."[37] There must be a way out. But what might it be?

The So-Called "Dependency Complex" of the Oppressed

Fanon will take us there . . . but not quite yet. He first enters into a critique of Octave Mannoni's *Prospero and Caliban: The Psychology of Colonialism*. Mannoni worked for a number of years in Madagascar and his book was one of the first attempts at applying psychology to a critique of colonialism (he later became part of the Lacanian school of psychoanalysis). Fanon appreciated his effort to examine the psychological dynamics of colonialism, but was not pleased with the results. The main problem is that Mannoni held that colonial subjugation in Madagascar did not result from social or economic forms of domination but rather from a "dependency complex" on the part of the natives. Traditional Malagasy culture is based on ancestor worship. They grow up feeling dependent on the Other—their ancestors—for their survival and self-identity. This produced in them, he claims, an "innate" dependency complex that they transferred onto the French colonialists when they occupied Madagascar in the late nineteenth century. A small number of colonialists were able to take over the island because the natives supposedly were already inclined to being conquered and dominated by them!

Fanon is fiercely critical of Mannoni, largely because he objects to the notion that colonialism is successful only where the natives suffer from an innate dependency complex. As is true of Sartre in *Anti-Semite and Jew*, he does not accept any approach that tries to explain domination on the basis of the "complexes" of its victims. Yet that is only part of Fanon's critique. He most of all takes issue with Mannoni's denial that various forms of ethnic and racial domination share a common structure. If colonialism in Madagascar is a result of the dependency complex of the natives, it follows that their domination is a special, exceptional case that cannot be used to explain the situation of those who lack such a dependency complex. Fanon, on the other hand, argues that, "colonial racism is no different from other racisms."[38] Anti-Jewish racism, Fanon insists, is not fundamentally different from anti-black racism. Nor are they different from any other kinds of racism. Fanon maintained to the end of his life that racism in the colonies does not have a different character or structure from racism in the "developed" Western world, including in the United States. Alice Cherki notes, "Fanon continued to hold on to the view he had divulged to Mannoni some years beforehand that there was no real difference between the day-to-day racism of the petty colonial settler and the racism of the metropolis. He would never veer from this position."[39]

Racism is not "produced" by some exceptional character structure or flaw on the part of its victims. Racism is produced by a structure of colonial and class domination that is wedded to specific socio-economic determinants. This is what makes it ubiquitous.

It is therefore no surprise that Fanon criticizes Mannoni for failing to see that racism and colonialism are "a reflection of the economic situation."[40] Mannoni was not wrong for trying to analyze the psychological implications of colonial domination. But by separating the latter from its socio-economic roots, he obscures the common structure that is found in all forms of racial discrimination.

It is worthwhile asking, why does Fanon spend so much time in the chapters on "The Woman of Color and the White Man" and "The So-Called Dependency Complex of the Colonized" on the socio-economic, when so much of what he wants to say is about the psychological? The reason is that focusing on the socio-economic locates the basis of racism in social reality. And if it is rooted in social reality, it is not a product of "human nature," biology, or "just the way things are." One of the deepest prejudices that many people harbor today is the myth that "racism has always existed" and that "everyone is by nature a racist." Fanon will have none of that. If racism is the product of some innate complex, an ontological structure, or "the human condition," it follows that racism can never be uprooted. All that becomes left is to affirm the "permanence of racism" as a given.[41] Fanon finds this approach to be completely unacceptable. He has no illusions about how hard it will be to eliminate racism. He is not entirely sure himself that a world of reciprocal recognitions will emerge in a world structured by racism. But he knows that it is not "being" that creates racism, but *society*, and since society is a creation of *human* beings, *what is made by us can also be unmade by us*. He writes

If [the black man] is overcome to such a degree by a desire to be white, it is because he lives in a society that makes his inferiority complex possible... it is to the extent that society creates difficulties for him that he finds himself positioned in a neurotic situation.[42]

Hence, the effort to change society will determine whether or not we will rid ourselves of the neuroses associated with racial domination. Fanon insists: "In no way must my color be felt as a stain . . . another solution is possible. It implies a restructuring of the world."[43]

The Hegelian Dialectic of Recognition

What is the pathway to achieving this? It may come as a surprise to learn that the philosophy that Fanon most relies upon to find a way out of this racist world is Hegel's. Hegel? The philosopher who denigrated the Africans for never having experienced history? The man who seemed to think that the white European constituted the *ne plus ultra* of history? Fanon undoubtedly knew of Hegel's misguided comments about Africa and Africans as well as his Eurocentrism, but that did not deter him from exploring the relevance of Hegel's dialectical *philosophy*. If Marx—to use a phrase of Alexander Herzen—considered Hegel's philosophy to be nothing less than "the algebra of revolution," *even while sharply critiquing his shortcomings*, why should Hegel not have something to teach us about how to reach a world of reciprocal recognitions?

Fanon's debt to Hegel is one of the most important philosophical influences in *Black Skin, White Masks*—if not in his thought as a whole—and this becomes clear from his reading of the *Phenomenology of Spirit*. Hegel's *Phenomenology* centers on the struggle of the subject to seek recognition through myriad stages of development—from the most initial phase, Consciousness, to Self-Consciousness, Reason, Spirit, Religion, and ultimately Absolute Knowledge. Each stage initially appears complete unto itself, but no sooner is each one reached than it turns out to be defective—until we reach Absolute Knowledge itself, the end of the separation of subject and object. The *Phenomenology of Spirit* is a development through contradiction, a "voyage of discovery" in which the subject struggles to overcome myriad forms of alienation on the way to freedom.

The first phase of the journey is *Consciousness*, in which the object posits itself as absolute—as what is independent of the subject. Objects seem to exist in-themselves, set off against the mind that knows them. It is the elemental, primary stage in which the world and the subject that perceives it are presumed to be totally independent entities. This "natural" or naïve standpoint soon shows itself to be inadequate, since the world that is known by consciousness is an act *of* consciousness. The assumption that the subject and object are cut off from each other by an impenetrable barrier becomes unsustainable.

Consciousness then gives way to the next stage, *Self*-consciousness, in which external objects lose their claim to independence; they are now objects *for me*. Self-consciousness is a somewhat unsettled stage, since on the one hand I am aware of myself as a subject and proud of it—but at the same time, I am aware of myself as an object, as a being of which others are aware. I claim to be at one with the world, but my very self-consciousness makes me aware of my distance from it. Self-consciousness craves unity, in that it tries to overcome the otherness of the external world; but the more it aims to do so, the more it becomes aware of the gap between otherness and itself. A sense of disquiet, even deep alienation, characterizes this stage. The subject is driven by a *desire* to negate this otherness of the external world by positing *itself* as absolute.

The duality within self-consciousness—its simultaneous sense of itself as a completed whole *and* as divided—creates a desire to negate or conquer the Other. This turns into a struggle onto death—a *violent* struggle, as each seeks to the annul the Other. This turns out to be fruitless, however, since desire needs an independent object to sustain itself; after all if there is no Other, there is nothing to be *desired*. The subject learns that it cannot satisfy itself by consuming or destroying the Other but must "achieve its satisfaction only in another self-consciousness."[44]

As a result, the subject now seeks *recognition* from the Other. There is nothing abstract about this struggle for recognition. It is not a clash between two disembodied minds. Each consciousness strives to achieve recognition from the Other by throwing its *body* into the fight. Self-consciousness is a *social* relationship. As one recent commentator on Hegel's *Phenomenology* puts it, "Self-consciousness craves unity . . . But there cannot be unity unless my self-consciousness is reconciled to my living body."[45] Hegel himself writes, "the object of immediate desire is a living thing [*lebendiges*]."[46] Anyone who presumes that the dialectic of Hegel's *Phenomenology* is a disembodied one will surely see little evidence of it in this section of the book.

The battle for recognition that Hegel is delineating should not be confused with liberal theories of recognition. The work of contemporary thinkers such as Alex Honneth, which treats recognition in terms of acknowledging social agents as citizens possessing equal political rights, has little to do with what Hegel is talking about—or what Fanon is interested in.[47] Recognition, for Hegel and Fanon, is about much more than a plea to be acknowledged as an equal citizen, or even as a living being. Hegel makes it clear that what each desires from the Other is recognition of the *dignity and worth* of its being. In other words, *I want to be recognized as absolute*—and so do you. This is far different from a mere acknowledgement of equality. On the contrary, Fanon contends

> By appealing, therefore, to our humanity—to our feelings of dignity, love, and charity—it would be easy to prove and have acknowledged that the black man is equal to the white man. But that is not our purpose. What we are striving for is to liberate the black man from the arsenal of complexes that germinated in a colonial situation.[48]

In Hegel's text, it soon becomes clear that the struggle unto death leads to failure, since if I kill the Other there is no one to provide me with recognition—and vice versa. The rival is therefore not killed off; he is instead made a slave. We have reached the famous master/slave dialectic. The master demands recognition from the slave, but since the master sees the slave as a non-essential being he feels no need to recognize him. The master is dominant, active and independent while the slave is submissive, passive and dependent. However, the subordinate position of the slave soon turns into its opposite. The slave fears the master, and this confirms, for the master, his dominance over him. Yet fear makes us aware of ourselves as sentient beings. By fearing the master the slave gets to know himself as an independent, essential being. Moreover, in his work the slave becomes conscious of his essentiality, since the master can't survive without him. The master tries to prove his *independence* by consuming the luxuries made by the slave, yet this only confirms his *dependence* upon the slave who makes them. Through this process the slave gets to discover his being-for-self. He develops an independent conscious-ness—*a mind of his own*—whereas the master possesses a dependent and miserable consciousness, which is lacking in any self-certainty of itself as an *active* subject.

Two things are evident in this much-discussed section of the *Phenomenology*. First, each phase immanently posits the absolute, even though each ultimately turns out to be defective. If the subject did not posit itself as an absolute it could not endure the battle for recognition. As Henri Lefebvre put it, "There is no moment except in so far as it embraces and aims to constitute an absolute . . . Liberty cannot make itself effective if it presents itself as arbitrary."[49] This absolute is not, however, fixed and frozen since, according to Hegel, the absolute is imbued with *negativity*. The act of positing itself as absolute manifests not only the subject's plenitude but also its incompleteness compared with further stages of development to come. In other words, the absolute exists *within* the relative; no sooner does it appear in a given phase than it appears incomplete. Hegel discusses the immanent—albeit *incomplete*—presence of the absolute within self-consciousness in the following terms:

With this we have before us the Notion of Spirit. What still lies ahead for consciousness is the experience of what Spirit is—this absolute substance which is the unity of the different independent self-consciousnesses which, in their opposition, enjoy perfect freedom and independence: the "I" that is "We" and "We" that is "I."[50]

Second, while the slave achieves a "mind of his own" in the battle for recognition, the effort to achieve mutual recognition turns out to be unsuccessful. The master is not overthrown at the end of the master/slave dialectic, nor does the master fully recognize the mind attained by the slave. *The struggle for recognition is still unresolved.* Reciprocal recognition does not begin to be truly reached until much later in the *Phenomenology*—in the chapter on Morality, which discusses the Christian conception of confession and forgiveness. As of the end of the master/slave dialectic, "Clearly, the slave does not do to the master what he does to himself, nor does the master do to himself what he does to the slave. Reciprocity is still incomplete. And so, mutual recognition, and the end of self-consciousness, has not yet been achieved."[51]

Fanon's Critical Recovery of Hegel's Dialectic

A careful reading of Fanon's text indicates that he has absorbed all of these concepts from the *Phenomenology of Spirit*. In chapter 7, "The Black Man and Recognition," he faithfully summarizes Hegel's discussion of the master/slave dialectic. He points out that self-consciousness requires recognition, but states that this is about more than just *acknowledging* the Other since "his *human worth* and reality depends on . . . his recognition by the Other."[52] He notes that this recognition must be mutual: "The Other . . . must perform a similar operation." He closely follows Hegel's notion that each phase of consciousness contains an immanent quest for the absolute: "Each consciousness of self is seeking absoluteness."[53] And he repeats Hegel's view that this is a struggle in which the subject *risks its life* to attain self-certainty—that is, *freedom*.

Fanon then states, in a crucial footnote, that when this master/slave dialectic is viewed in terms of race we get a very different *result* from what Hegel describes. Regardless of what Hegel did or didn't know of the history of black slavery and the revolts against it, such as the Haitian revolution,[54] it is clear that the historical context of Hegel's master/slave dialectic—more correctly translated as "lordship and bondage"—is the ancient and medieval world, in which slavery was *not* based on race.[55] This can hardly satisfy Fanon, since he is exploring Hegel to comprehend the *lived experience* of black people in the *contemporary* world. When the master/slave relation is viewed in terms of the additive of color, Fanon states that it becomes clear that the master is not interested in receiving recognition from the slave—whose very humanity he denies: "What [the master] wants from the slave is not recognition but work." But since no amount of labor can earn the slave recognition from the master *when the slave is black*, the slave's work fails to confirm his essentiality. Fanon concludes, "Therefore, he is less independent than the Hegelian slave."[56]

This has the following result: instead of gaining "a mind of *his own*," the black initially aspires for "values secreted by his masters."[57] The slave fails to attain the independent consciousness delineated by Hegel. Instead, the *black* slave seeks to gain recognition by trying to mimic the master and become white. Fanon has here provided a dialectical explanation for one of the central problems analyzed in his book—the tendency of the oppressed to interiorize their oppression, fall victim to an inferiority complex, and seek acceptance from the oppressor on its terms.

Fanon makes what may seem to be a surprising comment at the end of his discussion of the master/slave dialectic: "But the black man does not know the price of freedom because he has never fought for it."[58] This hardly seems an accurate accounting of the many slave revolts in which blacks *did* fight for freedom, such as the Haitian revolution. Fanon is clearly aware of this. He is not speaking of the experience of blacks in general but of what occurred in parts of the Lesser Antilles like Martinique, where they were given their freedom from above in 1848. As we saw in chapter 1, from as early as ten years old Fanon was distressed that the man who presumably "freed" the slaves—Schoelcher—was given all the credit, while the blacks got none. He is now applying this historical memory to a reading of Hegel. It is wrong, he is saying, to suggest that the blacks achieve recognition upon the immediate termination of the master/slave dialectic. Their human worth and subjectivity remain unrecognized. Hence, the negativity needed on the part of the former slave to surmount its position of subordination becomes all the sharper and more powerful.[59] Their struggle is not over; it must continue in permanence until freedom is achieved.

This is made manifest when Fanon states that the "*former* slave wants his humanity to be challenged; he is looking for a fight; he wants a brawl." He singles out the struggles of blacks in the U.S., "the twelve million black voices," who "have screamed against the curtain of the sky."[60] Faced with the failure of the end of slavery to lead to their recognition as human beings, they are compelled to take the fight further and deepen it—not by fighting for crumbs left on the table but by demanding from the Other the full, explicit, and complete recognition of their dignity as human beings.

It may seem that Fanon has departed radically from Hegel's analysis, and in one sense he has. However, it is worth noting—since the point tends to be overlooked by those who have not taken the trouble to seriously study Hegel's text—that in Hegel's account mutual recognition is *not* achieved at the end of the master/slave dialectic *even though the slave now has a "mind of his own."* Hegel says that no sooner does the slave gain an independent consciousness than he becomes aware of the gap between his subjectivity and the objective world, which remains to be transformed. A "mind of his own" that refrains from facing this reality, Hegel states, amounts to little more than "a piece of cleverness."[61] To reach mutual recognition, he shows, a longer and more complex road must still be traveled—one that does not end until we reach Absolute Knowledge itself!

Fanon *departs* from Hegel in denying that the black slave necessarily achieves an independent self-consciousness through his work, but in doing so he is in *accord* with Hegel's broader view that the struggle for recognition is not resolved at the rather provisional stage of the master/slave dialectic. This concept will in turn inform much of Fanon's later work, such as his critique of the pitfalls of national consciousness and the dangers of neocolonialism in *The Wretched of the Earth.*

The Particular and the Universal

We are not done with *Black Skin, White Masks*, since the question remains: if the additive of color indicates that an independent consciousness does not emerge from the master/slave dialectic, how does it come into being? Exactly how does the black subject overcome its inferiority complex and attain self-certainty of itself as a worthy and dignified being?

Fanon's entire book—one can even say his entire intellectual career—was driven by an effort to answer this question, but it is spoken to most directly in his dispute with Jean-Paul Sartre in the chapter entitled, "The Lived Experience of the Black Man."

Fanon has shown that racism so debases the human personality as to render mutual recognition impossible. It represents the "failure of man." This produces feelings of "rage . . . and an inadequacy in human communication that confine [the black person] into an unbearable insularity."[62] This can be manifested in various forms of anti-social behavior. So how is it overcome? He writes, "Since the Other was reluctant to recognize me, there was only one answer: to make myself known."[63] I must "shout my blackness"—express pride in the very socially constructed attributes of blackness that white society denigrates.[64] One would think that Fanon would have an ally here in Sartre, who wrote the introduction to one of the first collections of negritude poetry. Yet in *Black Orpheus*, Sartre refers to black consciousness and pride as a "weak stage" that must ultimately give way to the proletarian class struggle. Sartre contends, "the notion of race does not intersect with the notion of class."[65] For Sartre, race is a mere particular, class the universal.

Fanon is shocked; he feels betrayed. But he does not blame Hegel for Sartre's mistake. On the contrary, he turns Hegel *against* Sartre: "[T]his born Hegelian, had forgotten that consciousness needs to lose itself in the night of the absolute, the only condition for attaining self-consciousness."[66] Sartre has forgotten Hegel's most important insight—that the absolute is immanent in each phase, even though it makes its full appearance only at the end. The subject cannot endure the battle for recognition unless it posits its subjectivity as an absolute. Any effort to skip over that necessary moment leads to abstract revolutionism—an empty absolute. Black consciousness is not a "weak stage." Instead, Fanon insists, it is "an absolute density, full of itself."

> Still regarding consciousness, black consciousness is immanent in itself. I am not a potentiality of something; I am fully what I am. I do not have to look for the universal. There's no room for

probability inside me. My black consciousness does not claim to be a loss. It merges with itself.[67]

You must "lose yourself" in the particular in order to find your way to the universal. What Sartre forgot—and what many today still forget—is that "this negativity [of the black subject] draws its value from a virtually substantial absolutity."[68] Fanon never ceases to remind the reader that the *substantiality* of the black subject needs to be posited as an *absolute* in order to produce a viable pathway to freedom.

This perspective, drawn from his reading of Hegel, involves Fanon in a tricky navigation through the politics of negritude. It is negritude, after all, that Sartre had referred to as "a weak stage"—a mere phase on the way to the "true" revolutionary consciousness, *class* consciousness. Fanon is by no means uncritical of negritude in *Black Skin, White Masks*. He clearly feels discomfort with some of Senghor's statements—such as "emotion is Negro as reason is Greek."[69] It appears that many of the negritude poets are falling into precisely the kind of racial essentialism that Fanon has taken issue with in insisting there is no ontology of blackness. So why does he push back against Sartre by declaring "I needed to lose myself totally in negritude"?[70] Why does he do so even after calling much of negritude's espousal of black identity and an African past a "myth"? And why does he hold so firmly here to negritude, when he makes it clear—not just in this chapter, but in the book as a whole—that what he is striving for ultimately is not to be recognized as "black" or "African" but as a human being?

Ironic as it may sound, Fanon affirms the importance of negritude as the mediating term in the movement from the individual to the universal precisely because he *rejects* any black ontology. The obliteration of the subjectivity of the individual that is the function and aim of racism must be resisted, but the black subject has no fixed or biological essence to fall back upon in its attempt to do so. Its very "blackness," after all, is an arbitrary construction of the gaze of the white. The black subject therefore needs to construct an identity from a state of absence. Otherwise, the substantive power needed to endure and surmount the pain of living in a racialized world is out of reach. But *from what* is this identity to be forged? It has to come from *somewhere*. Just as substance is incomplete without subjectivity (Hegel's famous critique of Spinoza), subjectivity is incomplete when *shorn of* substance.[71] The substantiality comes, and must come, from the very notion of "blackness" contrived by white society. "Whether he likes it or not, the black man has to wear the livery the white man has fabricated for him."[72]

Fanon is concretizing Merleau-Ponty's insight (itself derived from the work of Husserl) that consciousness is not a free-floating signifier but is inseparable from the bodily-schema. Yes, I do not like how this society represents me in terms of my body; but since I can only know the world through the schema it has imposed upon it, I am compelled to engage the world on its basis. *However, I have made the decision to do so on my own terms*. The gaze of the Other has fixed me into this bodily-schema, but I am not merely an object. I am an *embodied subjectivity* that can act, move, and think—I do possess free will, even in being treated like an object, or being objectified. Your gaze has robbed me of my freedom, but I can only be robbed of something that I *have*.

On the other hand, if blackness is viewed as a minor term, as a mere phase on the way to get to something else, the subject will be robbed of access to the substantiality which can enable it to get to somewhere else—a world of mutual recognitions. Hence, "confronted with this affective ankylosis* of the white man, I finally made up my mind to shout my blackness . . . I secreted a race."[73] It may seem that Fanon is buying into the very myth of race that he seeks to overcome, and in one sense he is—although with a very large degree of self-awareness:

> I had rationalized the world, and the world had rejected me in the name of color prejudice. Since there was no way we could agree on the basis of reason, I resorted to irrationality. It was up to the white man to be more irrational than I. For the sake of the cause, I had adopted the process of regression, but the fact remained that

---

* Ankylosis is an abnormal stiffness of the joints. Fanon never ceases to emphasize the role of fixation in racial domination and classification.

it was an unfamiliar weapon; here I am at home; I am made of the irrational.[74]

Fanon has sought to engage the world as a rational being. But that world has not been welcoming. It has not reciprocated his rationality. Instead, an irrational force—white prejudice—has stopped him in his tracks. It is impossible to use reason to convince an irrational person of his fixation. But this does not mean that Fanon has embraced irrationalism. He well knows that "There is nothing more neurotic than contact with the irrational."[75] He accepts a temporary "regression" from rationality and embraces the mythos of negritude "for the good of the cause"—that is, to help provide the black subject with the confidence and self-assurance needed to take on a racist world. But he does so while not taking literally negritude's claims of having discovered an "authentic" black essence or genuine African culture. *He knows the latter is a myth.* He wants to be recognized as a human being and knows that the only way to achieve that is to demand that existing society accept his embodied subjectivity as it exists in-the-world.

Does this carry risks? Of course it does. Nothing is easier than to fall into a *fixed* particular—even as one argues against fixation. Black pride can readily become posed as an end-in-itself, just as can having pride in being a proletarian—even though the aim of human emancipation is to make both the proletariat and "blackness" superfluous. Sartre was not wrong to refer to racial pride and negritude as a particular. He was only wrong to treat the particular as a minor term. The difficult task is to navigate a route to the universal that neither skips over the particular nor becomes fixed in it.

Fanon posits black subjectivity as the mediating term to the universal, even in face of the risks that it entails, because otherwise it is not possible to obtain the recognition that victims of racism aspire for. You cannot ask to be accepted on "equal" terms with white society irrespective of race when this society has structured its very mode of seeing in racial terms. Fanon's insight that racism is a product of specific social relations that take on a life of their own is inseparable from his insistence that it is impossible to get to the "universal"—a world of genuine intersubjectivity—unless the particular is embraced and asserted without reservation, *as an absolute.*

This "absolute" does not signify some closed ontology. The "substantial absoluity" that Fanon speaks of is not free of negativity. *It is fully imbued with it.* And in this sense his view accords with at least one reading of Hegel, in which "the ceaseless movement of ideas and history" rather than *synthesis* is integral to what he means by "the absolute."[76] This is completely obscured by the vulgar notion that dialectics consists of some fixed movement of thesis-antithesis-synthesis—a view that has more to do with superficial readings of Hegel than anything Hegel himself wrote. Sekyi-Otu says the following of Fanon's understanding of Hegelian dialectical progression: "Nor does it have for its envisioned outcome the final goal of all vulgar dialectics: *synthesis*, the highest ambition of that fleeting and decorous 'moment of negativity' that is bourgeois nationalism . . . Fanon is anxious to capture the sense of new beginnings."[77]

How are these new beginnings reached? By grappling with the negativity found in your subordinate position, it becomes possible to discover the energizing force that takes you simultaneously *into* yourself and *out* of yourself. That is, by getting in touch with your negativity and by positing your subjectivity not as a minor term but as an absolute, you come closer to experiencing *absolute* negativity. And *this* is what enables you to be critical not just of the external enemy but your initial efforts to overcome it. Negativity "in general" is directed against *external* barriers to development; but *absolute* negativity calls into question the internal ones as well—including the internal barriers created by your own self. Once again, we see that the particular is the crucial mediating term in the dialectic of negativity. This journey to the universal though the particular is a difficult one to navigate, but it is the only way to ultimately break the chains of racism (with its accompanying tendencies toward self-hatred and self-denigration) and connect to the freedom struggles of others. As Fanon put it in his last book, "National Consciousness that is not nationalism is the only thing that will give us an international dimension."[78]

Fanon's overall philosophical approach in *Black Skin, White Masks* indicates that he is *breaking* with Hegel, insofar as Hegel did not construe the dialectic in terms of race and racism. Yet on another level he is *returning* to Hegel. It is a central Hegelian insight—perhaps the most important one in his entire philosophy—that the dialectical movement from individual to particular to universal (as well as in reverse) is a *necessary* one. Hegel was not of course thinking of the concerns Fanon had in mind in positing this logical syllogism at the heart of his philosophy. But that doesn't mean that it isn't just as imperative once the dialectic is reinterpreted in terms of Fanon's concerns.

We can sum up Fanon's approach as follows: He appropriates critical aspects of Hegel and Sartre's philosophy, albeit in opposite ways. He appropriates Sartre's view of distorted intersubjective relations in his *Being and Nothingness* insofar as it illuminates the nature of a racialized world, and this aspect of Sartre draws him away from Hegel. He appropriates Hegel's notion that genuine intersubjective communion with the Other can be achieved, and this aspect of Hegel draws him away from Sartre. The last thing that Fanon is doing is slavishly following his intellectual mentors. He is radically rethinking and revising their insights in terms of his lived experience.

The quest for the absolute explored by Fanon is no pursuit of a disembodied abstraction. It is the pursuit of what is most innermost to humanity—our human potential—which capitalism has alienated us from. What makes Fanon our contemporary is his understanding that any freedom struggle that does not posit a new humanism leads to a dead end—and the same is true of any effort to reach such a goal by skipping over the particular demands, struggles and subjectivities of specific forces of revolt. All the more reason then to turn anew to the dialectic, posit ourselves as an element of the contradiction, and navigate the difficult road that leads from the affirmation of the particular to the achievement of a new humanism.

3

The Engaged Psychiatrist: Blida and the Psychodynamics of Racism

In the period following the publication of *Black Skin, White Masks* in mid-1952, Fanon continued his psychiatric work at Saint-Alban. The book got relatively little attention; it only came to be considered a classic many years later. The few reviews that appeared were critical or dismissive—from the right, because of his sharp condemnation of Western society, and from the left, because of his unorthodox views concerning the path to overcoming racial discrimination. Even Sartre does not appear to have known of Fanon's work until years later (probably not until 1959). None of this deterred Fanon from continuing the experiments in socio-therapy that he was engaged in with Tosquelles at Saint-Alban. His main ambition at this point was pursuing a career in psychiatry at a public institution. He never appears to have considered working either in academia or in private practice.

In June 1953 Fanon sat for his examinations to qualify as a practicing psychiatrist (Le Médicat de Hopitaux Psychiatique), which he readily passed. The question then became where to go after Saint-Alban, where he had finished his residency. He had earlier (in February 1952) briefly returned to Martinique to look into the possibility of accepting a position at a hospital, but since it lacked a psychiatric facility he was uninterested. It was the last time he was to set foot in Martinique.

Back in France by September 1953, he took a position at Pontorson Hospital in La Manche, on the border of Normandy and

Brittany. Fanon was no doubt looking forward to implementing the techniques he had learned at Saint-Alban, but made little headway; the hierarchy resented his reforming zeal and he didn't get on well there. The provincial nature of La Manche also didn't suit him, and he lasted less than a month. Given that there were few opportunities for employment in major urban areas of France and that he had had enough of provincial life, he decided to seek employment elsewhere. His first choice was sub-Saharan Africa. He wrote to Senghor inquiring into the possibility of obtaining a position at a psychiatric hospital in Senegal, but got no response. After seeing an announcement for a job opening in Blida Algeria, he decided to take the position.

Fanon's Work at Blida-Joinville

Fanon's arrival in Algeria in November 1953 would prove to be the major turning point in his life, since within a relatively short time he was to become actively involved for the first time in an actual revolutionary movement. But it isn't as if he planned it that way. He did not go to Algeria to become involved in a national liberation struggle. The full-throttled emergence of the fight for independence was still a year away and Fanon knew little of Algerian politics at the time. He had been there before, as a soldier during World War II, so he was aware of France's brutal discrimination against the native Arab and Kabyle populace. Although the European minority (10 percent of the populace, large numbers of them not of French origin) monopolized political and economic power, many were farmers and workers—but still relatively privileged, since the per capita income of the Arab and Kabyle Muslims was $40 dollars a year (lower than the per capital GDP in China in 1949). Fanon had few illusions about the nature of Algerian society upon his arrival, but he went there to be a psychiatrist—not a committed political activist, though he most probably already favored Algerian independence from France. History is full of accidents and this would turn out to be a most intriguing one.

The Blida-Joinville Hospital is situated a few miles outside the town of Blida, 30 miles from Algiers. Fanon arrived knowing no Arabic, and his most immediate contacts were with Jews and left-wing Europeans critical of French colonialism. Fanon had always been keenly attentive to anti-Semitism and had many Jewish colleagues and friends. He never forgot the admonition of one of his philosophy professors from the Antilles who told him, "When you hear someone insulting the Jews, pay attention; he is talking about you." For Fanon, "the anti-Semite is inevitably a negrophobe."[1] Although Algeria's Jews (unlike the native Muslims) had been made French citizens in the late nineteenth century, there was plenty of anti-Semitism to be found. In addition to Algeria's homegrown fascists, many of the leaders and allies of the Vichy regime who were enthusiastic supporters of Nazi policies had moved to Algeria in the postwar years and comprised a significant part of its police force and administration. The European community was "racist from the top to bottom, regardless of sociocultural background."[2] Fanon had never directly encountered such a degree and extent of racism as in Algeria. It was not something that he had experienced in Martinique or even in metropolitan France. This must have had a profound impact on him personally, even if his prior work had prepared him to understand it intellectually.

Fanon became one of four doctors at Blida, which had 2,000 patients. It was the only facility in Algeria that treated long-term mental illness. He was not pleased by what he saw upon his arrival: patients treated like prisoners, Muslims walled off from Europeans, individual patients kept in isolation from one another. Fanon, who "was obsessed with the connection between human beings, the bond that can quash all differences"[3] set about reorganizing Blida around the principles of socio-therapy. Reports that Fanon unchained patients from their beds is probably apocryphal; he never mentions doing so and one of his colleagues denied that anyone had been in chains at Blida.[4]

In any case, there was plenty enough changes to make. In addition to his other responsibilities, Fanon was personally in charge of a ward of 164 European women and two-dozen Muslim males. Unlike at Pontorson no effort was made to prevent him from incorporating practices of institutional psychotherapy based on Tosquelles's approach. At his direction and urging, his colleagues introduced a series of dramatic changes. These included: Holding twice weekly meetings between doctors and patients to discuss the operation of the hospital, where patients were encouraged to speak their minds; establishing a weekly newspaper run by the patients; producing social and cultural events (including showing films and performing music) to encourage patients to interact with one another; and introducing occupational therapy to encourage productive activity. Many disciplinary restrictions were lifted and patients were allowed to roam around parts of the facility. These approaches may not seem that revolutionary today, but they were virtually unprecedented in Fanon's time—especially in hospitals in North Africa. Introducing these innovations, alongside therapeutic treatment of individual patients, took up a tremendous amount of Fanon's time and energy— twelve or more hours a day of work was not uncommon. When these and other practices were introduced in the ward housing European woman, the success rate in dealing with their problems and underlying illnesses increased considerably.

Things went differently went it came to treating the male Muslim patients. They did not take to the changes. The men disliked occupational therapy and disdained the idea of taking part in cultural events, holiday celebrations, and playing games with Europeans. Nor were they interested in participating in the newspaper. After three months of trying, Fanon called for a change of direction. He came to realize that approaches that worked for Westerners often did not for those from more traditional, Muslim cultures. In a paper co-written with his Blida colleague Jacques Azouley, he admitted, "We wanted to create institutions, but we forgot that any understanding of this kind must be preceded by a persistent, concrete, and genuine exploration of the foundations of the native society."[5] Tosquelles's socio-therapy could not so quickly be transplanted into an Algerian context without a careful consideration of such variables as the reluctance of Muslim men to participate in non-Muslim holidays and festivals and their distrust of social activities that they viewed as alien to their culture. As a result

It was necessary to alter perspectives, or at least to complete or carry out some elementary perspectives. It was necessary to attempt to seize the North African reality. It was necessary to require this "totality," in which Mauss sees the guarantee for an authentic sociological study. A leap had to be made, a transmutation of values had to be carried out. Let us admit it, it was necessary to go from the biological to the institutional, from natural existence to cultural existence.[6]

Fanon responded to this apparent setback by recognizing Muslim holidays and enabling patients to take part in commemorating them. Staff members were encouraged to learn Arabic so as to communicate directly with patients without the intermediary of a translator (Fanon himself took classes on Arabic, although he never became fluent in the language). Men were not put in the position of performing the kind of tasks that they might find culturally demeaning (this was especially related to specific forms of occupational therapy that women might be engaged in). Most important of all, an effort was made to better understand the specificity of Muslim religious and social practices rather than applying a single standard to the treatment of all patients.

New Insights on Mental Illness

As part of this effort, Fanon made a series of outings to Kabyle communities in the countryside in order to better understand their views of mental illness. These visits provided Fanon with a much richer understanding of Algerian society and culture than he possessed upon his arrival in 1953. He discovered that Kabyle culture tended to see the "insane" not as some kind of inherent threat or aberration but rather as individuals possessed by demons outside of their control. He co-authored a paper with François Sanchez that explored these issues in some detail. They wrote

It was not madness that inspired respect, patience, indulgence, it was man affected by madness, by genies; it was man as such. The attentive care that one lavishes on a tubercular patient, does it imply a particular sentiment vis-à-vis tuberculosis itself? Respect for the madman because he remains, in spite of everything, a man; and to the madman because he is subject to enemy forces.[7]

Respect for the dignity of man—including that of the madman—had clearly been one of the central motifs in Fanon's work since he began thinking about the intersection between philosophy and psychology. At Blida he now had the chance of developing this further by engaging in careful studies of actual indigenous practices. Philosophical generalizations were being further fleshed out, and in some case revised, through empirical, scientific analyses of native conditions.

This concern was also reflected in an unpublished paper written with Azouley and Sanchez on sexual disfunctionality among North African males. It discusses how Muslims generally did not visit a European doctor or clinic to deal with such problems but consulted a Muslim religious teacher or *taleb*. Their culture likewise viewed such issues not as a sign of illness but an affliction resulting from acts of magic. Fanon, Azouley and Sanchez acknowledged that "Islamic society is a theocratic society and there is no room in it for secularism" and that elders and religious figures play a prominent role.[8] But they did not allow this criticism to overshadow the positive cultural contributions. As one study puts it

> What makes it significant is the fact that the authors take the practices they are describing so seriously and that they obviously listened to their *taleb* with great respect. The word "superstititon" was never used. The *taleb* . . . [is] clearly regarded as being in possession of a coherent body of knowledge and a diagnostic system that makes sense in its own terms. Understanding that knowledge and that system was a way of coming to terms with problems the authors encountered in their psychiatric practice, because it enabled them to grasp their patients' own understanding of their sexual problems.[9]

The papers co-authored with Azouley and Sanchez are but three of 15 papers on psychiatry that Fanon wrote and/or co-authored with others over the course of his career. It is a shame that none of these have been published in English translation and most are difficult to access. They enable us to see the extent to which his psychiatric and philosophical concerns are intertwined and developed in new ways following the publication of *Black Skin, White Masks*.[10]

A particularly fascinating paper was written in 1955 with R. Lacaton, another colleague at Blida, entitled "Confessions in North Africa." It focuses on the role of confession in Algerian society and its relationship to overcoming the separation between the individual and the community. Hussein Abdilahi Bulhan writes of this in his study of Fanon's psychological writings:

> Ordinarily, the authors argued, confession for wrongdoing has both existential and social dimensions, a private as well as a public import. Existentially, confession implies a willingness to assume personal responsibility and, in so assuming, to affirm the meaning of one's being revealed through the act. Not to assume such responsibility for one's action or to falsely deny it is to experience a fundamental alienation of one's being, at least in that moment. Socially, confession indicates that an "auto-condemnation" has been provoked in the conscience, that the values and ethical precepts of the community, if not already internalized, are now reinstalled in the actor.[11]

Their paper argued that confession is a form of mutual interaction that helps overcome a lack of recognition between individuals. Although Hegel is nowhere mentioned in the piece—there would seem to be no reason to do so, given that it is a paper on psychiatry and not philosophy—their discussion has a striking resonance with the discussion of recognition in the *Phenomenology of Spirit*. As noted in chapter 2, mutual recognition is not truly achieved in the master/slave dialectic. It attains a fuller actualization much later in the "journey of discovery" that constitutes the *Phenomenology*—in Hegel's discussion of conscience and confession. Hegel states

> The forgiveness which [the confessing consciousness] extends to the other is the renunciation of itself, of its unreal essential being . . . The word of reconciliation is *objectively* existent Spirit, which beholds the pure knowledge of itself qua universal essence, in its opposite, in the pure knowledge of itself *qua* absolutely

self-contained and exclusive *individuality*—a reciprocal recognition which is *absolute* Spirit.[12]

It is impossible to say whether Fanon had Hegel in mind in composing the paper on confession, but it surely seems to conform to the *concepts* found in Hegel himself.

Throughout his work at Blida, Fanon was particularly attentive to the specific forms by which racial oppression structures the behavior and attitudes of its victims as well as perpetrators. At the same time, he was interested in the possibilities of engendering subjective growth and resistance among the subjugated. He wrote

The oppressor, through the inclusive and frightening character of his authority, manages to impose on the native new ways of seeing and in particular judgment with respect to his original form of existing. This event, which is commonly designated as alienation, is naturally very important. It is found in the official texts under the name of assimilation.

This process, however, fails to completely reduce the subject to an objectified state or eradicate its ability to resist: "Now this alienation is never wholly successful. Whether or not it is because the oppressor qualitatively and quantitatively limits the evolution, unforeseen, disparate phenomena manifest themselves."[13]

The task of the clinician is to make these "disparate phenomena" less unforeseen, by encouraging activities and discussions among patients that can help elicit from them a different mental horizon than the one imposed by colonialism. This is a difficult task, since "It is not possible to enslave men without logically making them inferior through and through. And racism is only the emotional, affective, sometimes intellectual explanation of this inferiorization."[14] But while racism obeys a "flawless logic" that defines a society and culture from top to bottom, it is "not a constant of the human spirit." It is possible to awaken "an absolute valorization almost in defiance of reality."[15] More and more, Fanon is stressing the importance of being overdetermined from without in order to comprehend the pathway toward achieving disalienation from within.

The Process of Disalienation

In this sense, Fanon's critique of psycho-affective disorders has some parallels with Marx's critique of capital. Marx's *Capital*, though rooted in economics, consists of more than a mere economic description of capitalist phenomena. Its actual aim is to trace out the objectified, reified form of human praxis in societies governed by a capitalist mode of production. It delineates the odyssey of capital, this mysterious objectified form that seems to take on a life of its own. Capital is congealed abstract labor, the objectified form of undifferentiated human labor power. Since the object, dead labor, dominates the subject, living labor, human relations *appear* to take on the form of relations between things because that is what they *really are*. By tracing out the development and tendency towards dissolution of this objectified form, Marx's *Capital* is adequate to its subject matter—a society in which the object dominates the subject. And yet it is precisely the analysis of this objectified, alienated expression of human praxis that discloses its absolute opposite— humanity's capacity for freely creative, purposeful activity when *freed* from the capital relation. Marx refers to this as the realm in which "human power is its own end."[16] The delineation of objectified forms does not therefore only reveal the contours of alienation, but also the quest for new human relations that are buried *within* it. In at least one crucial sense, Fanon is doing something very different. He is trying to delineate the objectified form that human praxis assumes in a colonized society by investigating its impact on the human psyche. While he constantly stresses that the *basis* of racism is socio-economic, he is committed to exploring its *inner* life in the subject. In doing so, he delineates the objectified form of the psyche, its formative power in shaping, and misshaping, the being of the individual subjected to the gaze of the Other. And he does so in such a way as not only to reveal the contours of alienation but also the quest for new human relations by the subject who resists it. *Alienation, as he sees it, is "never wholly successful."* Marx and Fanon are working on very different levels and there is no one-to-one relation or homology between their respective projects. Nevertheless, what binds the two together is that they proceed *from* a phenomenological analysis of reification *to* an articulation of its absolute opposite—the quest for a new humanism.

Ironically, what many post-Marx Marxists do to Marx is what many postcolonial theorists do to Fanon: they focus on his analysis of the overdetermining power of alienation and repression in his critique of existing society and culture while passing over his humanism. Fanon's sensitivity to cultural difference and contingency is celebrated, while his advocacy of a "New Humanism" is often treated as a naïve hangover from the heritage of the European Enlightenment. Yet it is difficult, if not impossible, to come to grips with Fanon's work in psychiatry without being attuned to its profound humanist content. As Alice Cherki insightfully argues

> Difference, in the hands of the culturalists, is posited as a challenge to the universalism that informs the great systems of Western knowledge. Fanon, on the other hand, views culture as a point of temporal and spatial reference that is also a conduit to the universal . . . Fanon was a helpless believer in humankind.[17]

Fanon's practice of psychiatry was unconventional in many respects, but that does not mean that he neglected the role of more standard approaches. He did not subscribe to the view that mental illness is a mere illusion created by a self-interested medical establishment; for him, it was an objective reality, produced by an alienated society. He never refers to mental illness as a "myth." He endorsed the use of electroshock and antidepressants (such as lithium citrate) and discussed their impact in a number of his psychiatric writings. It was not the use of specific techniques that defined his work as much as the goal to which they were directed. David Macey captures this as follows:

> Fanon consistently described mental illness as a form of alienation from the world and as a loss of existential freedom. As a therapist, his goal was to "consciousnessize" (*conscienciser*) his patient's conflicts so as to establish a new and more positive relationship with the external world. Fanon always stresses the sociogenic aspects of symptomatology: symptoms did not, in his view, originate from

the person's unconscious or repressed sexual impulses as much as from a distorted dialectic between the ego and the world and from the internalization of social conflicts.[18]

As noted earlier, this does not mean that Fanon took issue with the determinative importance of the unconscious. At issue is the etiology of the unconscious, not its existence. He understood that individuals are often shaped by a collective unconscious that predetermines their choices and commitments. But the specific forms of unconscious behavior he was primarily interested in—the psycho-affective disorders associated with racism—cannot be properly understood in terms of an *a priori* form or archetype. This standpoint is what drove the formulation of many of his therapeutic practices at Blida and elsewhere.

Fanon continued to experiment with different treatments and approaches. He discovered over time more effective means of providing treatment to his Muslim patients, though it took a considerable amount of trial and error. He continued to challenge the prison-like character of mental institutions by embarking on such projects as building a theater and soccer stadium for inmates, creating a school for nurses, and introducing an open clinic for those suffering from mild cases of mental illness. One cannot help but be struck by the enormous amount of care and attentiveness with which Fanon directed to the transformation of the institution. This work was to be cut short, however, by factors outside of his control—the heating up of the war of liberation against the French.

The Development of a New Psychiatric Perspective

The pivotal moment was November 1, 1954—when the newly formed Front for National Liberation (FLN) initiated an armed uprising for independence. Few things were to be the same again in Algeria or in Fanon's life. He was quickly drawn into the independence struggle—though not yet openly. Although he considered joining the *maquis* as a fighter in 1955, he never did so. He was much more valuable to the FLN as a practicing psychiatrist who treated resistance fighters in Blida and hid many of them on its premises from the French Army.

Fanon's work at Blida-Joinville was transformed, in many respects, by the increasingly desperate nature of the French effort to hold onto Algeria in the aftermath of the events of November 1954. An increasing number of his patients were victims of the carnage unleashed by the French military crackdown. Many of his patients were civilians who had been brutally tortured by the French and were suffering severe psychic disorders as a result. Others had seen family members "disappear" or murdered and were suffering from severe depression or suicidal tendencies. Many of those that he treated (often with anti-depressant medications) were FLN militants who were suffering from what we now refer to as post-traumatic stress disorder. At the time, the impact of warfare and systematic violence upon the human psyche was neither a widespread topic of discussion nor a central concern of much of the clinical literature on mental illness, but Fanon's work can be viewed as anticipating more recent understandings of post-traumatic stress disorder—especially since the 1990s. Fanon discusses a number of specific cases reflecting the problem in both in his clinical writings and books (such as *A Dying Colonialism* and *Wretched of the Earth*). In a number of instances, he also treated members of the French paramilitaries who came to Blida-Joinville because of the assortment of ailments associated with their work as "professional" torturers for the French authorities. Fanon did not choose his patients based on their political background or affiliation; such a notion would have been anathema to him.

Fanon's activities were closely watched by the French authorities, and by the end of 1956 the intensification of repression against all real and perceived supporters of Algerian independence made it impossible for him to remain at Blida. He resigned and was forced to go into exile, in Tunisia, at the beginning of 1957. But that did not mark the end of Fanon's work as a practicing psychiatrist. He went on to work at several other hospitals in Tunisia, even as he emerged as a major spokesperson for the FLN and the African revolutions as a whole.

The next chapter will explore Fanon's relationship with the FLN and the Algerian revolution. What needs to be noted here is that just as Fanon's practice of psychiatry lead him deeper into direct revolutionary politics, his involvement in revolutionary politics impacted his work as a psychiatrist. He first took a part-time position at Razi Hospital in Manouba and went to work trying to transform the institution along the lines of what he done at Blida. The locks came off the doors, patients were encouraged to socialize with one another, and other reforms were attempted to humanize the institution. But Fanon faced less success than at Blida, largely because of the fierce objections from its director Dr. Ben Soltan, who reeked of anti-Semitism and anti-black racism (Soltan actually accused Fanon of being a "Zionist agent"; his colleagues in the FLN refuted the charge, which hardly anyone took seriously).

Fanon was forced to leave Manouba and began to work at Charles-Nicolle General Hospital in Tunis. Unlike the experience at Manouba, he was accepted by his colleagues at Charles-Nicolle and quickly established a reputation there. His foremost accomplishment was introducing a neuropsychiatric day-care clinic. No day clinic for the mentally ill existed anywhere else in Africa at time, though a few operated in Europe. Its formation marked an important shift in Fanon's thinking and practice.

Fanon had come to the conclusion that the effort to create a kind of society-in-miniature in a psychiatric clinic—a practice that he learned directly from Tosquelles—had its limitations. The patient was still walled off from the rest of society, even if the conditions inside the facility were less alienating and repressive. The division between clinical treatment and everyday life persisted. Creating a neuropsychiatric day-care clinic moved things in a different direction. Patients could come in for treatment without losing their connections with their families, friends, and society at large. This marked a revolutionary break, not just from standard practice, but also from much of what Fanon had been doing earlier. By the time he got to Tunisia, and thanks in large part to his increasingly intense involvement in revolutionary politics, Fanon was going beyond what he learned from Tosquelles. He was now envisioning a breaking down of the walls that separate psychiatric care from the everyday life outside of the clinic or hospital.

This did not represent the end of Fanon's work as a psychiatrist. He practiced psychiatry at no less than seven different institutions in the late 1950s. He also gave lectures on psychiatry at the University of

Tunis, in 1958 and 1959, for both interns and militants interested in psychology. At least a portion of the lectures dealt with the effect of neuroses on factory workers. David Macey suggests that "Fanon was becoming much more interested in social and industrial psychology than in any form of Freudianism."[19]

The notion that Fanon "abandoned" psychiatry and psychology upon becoming an active revolutionary has no basis. On the contrary, he intended to return to a psychiatric practice in Algeria following its achievement of national independence. But that was not to be, since the trajectory of the revolution, and his life, led to a very different outcome.

4

The Engaged Philosopher: The FLN and the Algerian Revolution

There can be little doubt that the event that crystallized the nature of French colonialism in Algeria, as well as the response to it by its native populace,* occurred on May 8, 1945. It was the day of the infamous Sétif massacre of 30,000 Algerians by "Free French" troops. It occurred on the very day that World War II ended in Europe. What began as a march of 5,000 Algerians to celebrate the end of the war turned into a massacre extending over five days and extending into several neighboring towns and villages, as French forces brutally attacked the populace for having raised demands for independence from France. The police, accompanied by the Foreign Legion and the French Air Force and Navy, brutally and indiscriminately attacked civilian areas in an effort to make it clear that France's liberation from German occupation would in no way signal the liberation of Algeria from French occupation. Few around the world who were celebrating the victory over Nazism that month were probably paying much attention to what happened at Sétif (including in France itself), but that was surely not the case in Algeria.

The French authorities no doubt thought that the massacre had crushed the nascent calls for independence, since in the following years things seemed fairly quiet. Faced with brutal repression, the advocates of independence dispersed, went underground, or fled to the hills to begin organizing armed resistance. But the initial bands of

---

* I am referring here to Algeria's non-European residents, not the Europeans who had resided there since it became a French colony.

guerrillas were small and relatively isolated, and the cities remained calm. The French authorities clearly had the upper hand. But this was nothing compared with the silence in France, where Sétif and its aftermath were barely discussed. A French colony since 1830, Algeria was in the unique position of being considered an integral part of France by virtually every political tendency in the country. So ubiquitous was the view that "Algeria is and forever shall be French!" that even the communist PCF denounced the Sétif protesters as "provocateurs" while refraining from condemning the massacre of 30,000 people—many of whom were brutally tortured to death.

When Fanon arrived in Algeria in 1953, there was little evidence of an active independence movement and none of the other African colonies had yet achieved political independence. But the idea of independence was in the air. These were the heady years of decolonization around the world in the aftermath of the independence of India, Indonesia, and China's successful national revolution of 1949. Fanon knew little about Algerian politics at the time and was not in direct contact with those who would later (at the end of 1954) form the FLN. He did make contact with the Association of Algerian Youth for Social Action (AJAAS), group of Muslim and European youth opposed to colonialism, soon after his arrival. But political activism was not yet his main concern; he had his hands full introducing the techniques of socio-therapy at Blida. Unbeknownst to Fanon at the time, the mole of history was nevertheless doing its work, since exiled activists, guerrilla fighters and urban residents opposed to French colonial rule were preparing an insurrection.

The Algerian National Liberation Movement

The explosion of a series of bombs in Algiers on November 1, 1954, which occurred at the same time as the announcement of a new political formation responsible for them, the Front de Libération Nationale (FLN), shocked the French authorities.[1] It also deeply impacted Fanon; things were never to be the same again.

The FLN has always presented the events of November 1, 1954 as ground zero of the revolution, conveniently (and willfully) ignoring the many earlier nationalist organizations that had arisen in opposition to French colonial policies. Some of these, such as the North-African Star (headed by Messali Hadj)—Algeria's first modern nationalist organization—came into existence as far back as the 1920s. The Party of the Algerian People (PPA), its successor organization, was founded in the late 1930s and by 1947 grew into the Democratic Movement for the Triumph of Algerian Freedom (MTLD). Other groups were also on the scene by then, such as Ferhat Abbas's Union for the Algerian Manifesto (founded in 1946), which sought Franco-Muslim cooperation instead of immediate independence. (The Algerian Communist Party was formed in 1920 as an extension of the PCF, but it opposed independence until the mid-1950s and was not taken seriously by the national liberation movement.) It was not as if the fight for Algerian independence began on November 1, 1954, when the FLN made its entrance into history.[2] To Fanon, however, the FLN's claim to be its progenitor made perfect sense since from the vantage point of *his* lived experience November 1, 1954 *was* ground zero of the revolution.

Although France considered Algeria an integral part of France, the native Arab and Kabyle populace were prevented from having any effective political or economic power. A so-called Algerian National Assembly came into existence in 1947, but it was a farce: one European ballot counted for nine Muslim votes. The European minority was a diverse group, descending from migrants not just from France but also from many other parts of Europe, but their political and economic privileges placed them in a different world from the native Muslim populace. This had been the case since the mid-nineteenth century, a process that was spelled out graphically by Rosa Luxemburg in *The Accumulation of Capital*:

Alongside the martyrdom inflicted upon British India, the history of French policy in Algeria can claim a place of honor in the annals of capitalist colonial economies. When the French conquered Algeria [in 1830], prevalent among the masses of the Arab-Kabyle population were ancient social and economic forms of organization that had persisted, in spite of the long and turbulent history of the country, until the nineteenth century, and indeed these continue to exist to some degree even today . . .

Yet French policy in Algeria was a pole of constancy throughout this series of phenomena; from beginning to end, it was oriented toward a single goal, and it revealed more clearly than anything else that all of these transformations of the political regime in nineteenth century France revolved around one and the same fundamental interest—i.e. the dominance of the capitalist bourgeoisie and its form of property.[3]

One might have expected that the full-scale emergence of a movement for national independence would have led some on the French political scene to lend a friendly ear to the struggle, but that was not the case in 1954—and for many years afterward. The French Interior Minister at the time was François Mitterrand, the Socialist Party leader who later became French President, in 1981; he denounced the uprising in the harshest of terms and insisted that Algeria remain French. The communists grouped in the PCF were no better. It supported France's effort to maintain control of Algeria—a position that was not contested at the time (or much later) by such leading PCF theorists as Louis Althusser. Things got only worse from there: in 1956 Guy Mollett's "Socialist" government, with the support of the PCF, voted emergency powers that effectively imposed martial law in Algeria. Tens of thousands were rounded up and tortured to death (many of the techniques used by the French would later be picked up by the U.S. in its "war on terror"). The worst kind of fascistic excesses was exacted upon the rebels—and innocent civilians—by the French forces. It would be a long time before France agreed to give up control of Algeria. In the next eight years 27,000 French troops and over a million native Algerians would die in the war (the latter figure exceeds the percentage of Frenchmen killed in World War I).

To this day, the extent of France's murderous war against the Algerian movement for independence—one that was compelled to take up arms by the 1950s because of the extent of French repression—is largely ignored or conveniently forgotten by much of the French public. This is not unconnected with the tendency of much of French society, including some on the left, to deny the critical importance of race in shaping social relations. As one indigenous rights activist and theorist in France recently wrote, "The French radical Left has never felt comfortable with the 'race' concept and has long seen racism as just 'bad ideas' or as a 'simple' obstacle against the unity of workers."[4] Such conceptual blindspots have often dovetailed with the failure of all-too-many to keep in mind that the terror that France imposed upon Algeria from 1954 to 1962 represents one of the gravest crimes against humanity of the twentieth century.

First Contacts with the FLN

It appears that Fanon and the FLN contacted each other a few months after November 1954. It was the FLN who first contacted him—not the other way around. They did not seek him out because of his reputation as a writer or political thinker (Fanon's writings were virtually unknown in Algeria at the time). The FLN was looking for a psychiatrist to help its recruits deal with mental problems. Pierre Chalet, an Algerian of European origin who worked at Blida as a specialist in tuberculosis and had contacts with the resistance (he was active in AJAAS and a supporter of Algerian independence), recommended that the FLN get in touch with Fanon. It was therefore through his work as a physician that Fanon was first brought into the orbit of nationalist politics.[5]

As was typical of Fanon, once the contact was made he threw himself wholeheartedly into the cause. He was not one to make partial commitments and neutrality was always out of the question for him. In early 1955 he contemplated joining the guerrillas in the Aurès Mountains, but never did so; the FLN needed him for more important tasks at Blida, as Fanon well understood. By February 1955, FLN representatives were secretly meeting with him in his offices in Blida to arrange for militants to be housed at the hospital (this included wounded fighters getting medical treatment). Initially, he had close ties with FLN commander Slimane Dehilés (aka Colonel Saddek), who was considered part of the Marxist wing of the FLN.

In February 1955 Fanon published an essay in the French journal *Esprit* that points to a subtle shift in some of his views—possibly due to events in Algeria. The essay, "West Indians and Africans," reprises some of the themes of *Black Skin, White Masks* (a work he explicitly mentions). He writes, "The truth is that there is nothing, *a priori*, to warrant the assumption that such a thing as a Negro people exists" and adds, "questions of race are but a superstructure, a mantle, an obscure ideological emanation concealing an economic reality."[6] He notes that whereas prior to World War II West Indians denied their African roots, this changed with negritude: "Then it became real that not only the color black was invested with value, but fiction black, ideal black, black in the absolute, primitive black, the Negro."[7] This affirmation, he adds, did not resonate with African reality, where "the native, the black, the dirty, was rejected, despised, cursed. There an amputation had occurred; there humanity was denied." He concludes, "It thus seems that the West Indian, after the great white error, is now living in the great black mirage."[8] This points to a more critical stance toward negritude than voiced in his earlier writings. It may be due to the fact that while Algerians were taking up arms for independence, leading negritude poets like Césaire were arguing for Martinique to remain a part of France. From this point onward Fanon become increasingly distant from Césaire and the negritude movement as a whole.

In August 1955 the FLN launched a full-scale insurrection. The French responded by widening and intensifying its repression. A "Manichaean" divide showed itself between colonizers and colonized—a term that Fanon uses as early as *Black Skin, White Masks*[9] and which is further developed in *The Wretched of the Earth*. A few months later Fanon conveyed his thoughts about the Algerian situation to Daniel Guérin, the French anarchist writer and gay activist

Every passing hour is an indication of the gravity and imminence of the catastrophe . . . Algerian territory will run with blood. Armed with their knowledge of the natives, the Europeans are planning to punish suspects and sympathizers at once . . . We are receiving information about summary executions from many regions. The days to come will be terrible days for this country. European civilians and Muslim civilians are really going to take up the gun. And the bloodbath no one wants to see will spread across Algeria.[10]

The Soummam Conference of 1956

The year 1956 was a crucial one, both for the Algerian revolution and Fanon's relationship to it. At the time of its public emergence at the end of 1954 the FLN had issued a statement of its aims and objectives, but this co-called Roneoed Proclamation was rather vague about ideology, structure, and ultimate goals. Internal divisions about the form and direction of the group were already surfacing, so in August 1956 the FLN held a clandestine conference in the Soummam Valley to further clarify its positions. It proved to be enormously important—including for Fanon. In the course of three weeks of debate it specified the role of the armed wing of the FLN, the Armeé de la Libération (ALN), mandating that the political leadership take precedence over military commanders. It stipulated that the "forces of the interior" (that is, those inside Algeria) take priority over those outside the country. And it mandated that decisions be made on a collective, democratic basis and binding on all members. It also emphasized the need to gain support for its cause in France and promised equal rights to the Jewish and European minority after independence. Other aspects of what would happen after liberation were left vague; although the Soummam Declaration proclaimed the need for a "democratic social republic," "socialism" was not mentioned. It also made no mention of a future religious state. The tensions within the FLN, between its more radical secular-socialist elements and those preferring an Arab-Islamic state, was left to be decided for another day.

The driving force behind the conference was Ramdane Abane, a secular socialist who had become the FLN's main organizer in Algiers in 1955. Fanon was not at Soummam—there was no reason for him to be since at the time he was nowhere near the center of power in the FLN—but he became very close with Abane and in many respects considered him his political mentor. Although Abane's insistence on the priority of the political over the military wing of the movement propelled him to the top leadership of the FLN after the Soummam Conference, he soon found himself embroiled in disputes with military commanders and others in the FLN for what he considered their authoritarianism and lack of a vision of the future.

According to Ferhat Abbas, a moderate who led Algeria's provisional government in exile, the GPRA, from 1958 to 1961, Abane told the military commanders on one occasion, "You have created a power that is based on military might, but politics are another matter and cannot be conducted by illiterates and ignoramuses." Referring to them on another occasion, he said, "They embody the exact opposite of the freedom and democracy we want for an independent Algeria . . . Algeria is not the Orient where absolute potentates can rule unchallenged."[11] Fanon was probably not conscious of such divisions within the FLN at the time of the Soummam Conference, but he became aware of them in due time and Abane's perspective was the one that he most closely identified with.

Racism and Culture

Not long after the Soummam Conference, in September 1956, Fanon attended the First World Congress of Black Writers and Artists in Paris. Organized by *Présence africaine*, it brought together delegates from two-dozen countries, including Richard Wright from the U.S., Césaire from the West Indies, and Senghor and Alioune Diop from Africa. Fanon had not yet publicly declared himself a supporter of the FLN—that would have seriously jeopardized the safety of his colleagues and made it impossible to continue his work at Blida— but he must have been disappointed to find that there was virtually no mention of Algeria or its independence movement by the other attendees. This did not deter him from delivering a speech that reflects what he was learning from his Algerian experience.

Fanon's speech, entitled "Racism and Culture," is one of his great creative achievements. It explores "the consequences of racism on the cultural level." He states, "The object of racism is no longer the individual man but a certain form of existing." Yet there are different forms or expressions of racism:

> Vulgar racism in its biological form corresponds to the period of crude exploitation of man's arms and legs. The perfecting of the means of production inevitably brings about a camouflage

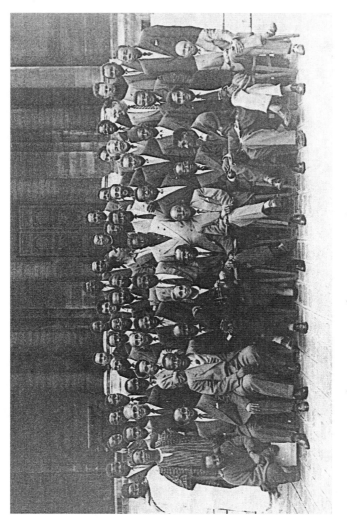

Figure 2   Participants at the First Congress of Negro Writers and Artists in Paris, 1956. Fanon is in third row from front, second from left.

of the techniques by which man is exploited, hence of the form of racism.[12]

Contemporary colonialism represents this latest effort at "camouflaging." Europe tries to conceal its exploitation of the colonized by reminding everyone of the "democratic principles" that is it based upon. Yet the native who is initially drawn, because of his inferiority complex, toward the colonial power, soon discovers that "every colonialist is a racist"—regardless of the "universal" principles that they espouse.[13] As a result, "tradition is no longer scoffed at by the group. The group no longer runs away from itself. The sense of the past is rediscovered, the worship of ancestors resumed."[14] It may seem that Fanon is here reprising many of the themes associated with negritude that he had discussed in *Black Skin, White Masks.*

However, toward the end of the speech Fanon's tone undergoes a radical shift. It becomes decidedly more political:

No neologism can mask the new certainty: the plunge into the chasm of the past is the condition and the source of freedom. The logical end of this will to struggle is the total liberation of the national territory. In order to achieve this liberation, the inferiorized man brings all his resources into play, all his acquaintances, the old and the new, his own and those of the occupant. The struggle is at once total, absolute.[15]

The *total* liberation of the national territory . . . now posed as an *absolute.* Fanon is uncompromising in his support for national liberation. As in *Black Skin, White Masks* the mediating term in the movement from the particular to the universal—the effort to affirm consciousness of self in the face of racism—is posed as an absolute. However, this mediating term is now concretely expressed as a *mass movement* aspiring for self-assertion. He makes this explicit in stating

A people that undertakes a struggle for liberation rarely legitimizes race prejudice. Even in the course of acute periods of insurrectional armed struggle one never witnesses the recourse to biological justifications. The struggle of the inferiorized is situated on a markedly more human level. The perspectives are radically new. The opposition is the henceforth classical one of the struggles of conquest and of liberation.[16]

The biological view of race that is still echoed, in part, in negritude, is supplanted by an *embodied* subjectivity—masses in motion—that tries to reclaim the dignity of the black individual. A "classical" struggle of forces engaged in *actual* combat—colonizer versus the colonized—replaces the abstract call to forge some mythical identity based on epidermal considerations. *There will be a fight to the finish between those struggling for national independence and those opposing it.* This does not infer that Fanon has forgotten about the universal. He concludes, "universality resides in this decision to recognize and accept the reciprocal relativism of different cultures, once the colonial status is irreversibly excluded."[17]

Fanon's speech does not appear to have received much discussion at the conference. Perhaps his explicit advocacy of "armed struggle" was one of the reasons. In addition, the other delegates could not have failed to notice his implicit criticisms of negritude. In any case, he did not restrict himself to discussions at the conference. While in France he also made time to meet with Jean Ayme, a Trotskyist militant, and spent many hours discussing politics with him as well as Pierre Broué, the historian of the European workers' movements. Fanon's encounter with Ayme was not ephemeral. They took a great liking to each other (Ayme was also a psychiatrist) and on a visit to France several months later Fanon stayed several weeks at his home. At that time Ayme gave him the transcripts of the first four congresses of the Communist International, which reportedly held "a great fascination for Fanon."[18] Fanon was no doubt intrigued at the efforts of the pre-Stalinist communist movement of the early 1920s to establish connections with the anti-colonial movements in Asia and the Middle East.[19]

Important Shifts in World Politics

Fanon no sooner returned to Algeria than two events occurred which he viewed as defining moments of world politics. One was the

Hungarian revolution of October 1956. The other, which occurred virtually simultaneously, was the Franco-British-Israeli invasion of Suez. Fanon saw the Suez invasion as a desperate attempt to maintain France's colonial domination of Algeria (Egyptian President Gamal Abdel Nasser had come out in support of the FLN). Although the invasion proved to be a fiasco—the British, French, and Israelis were forced to withdraw under U.S. pressure—Fanon took it to mean that a long and hard struggle was ahead for the independence movement. He had earlier hoped that the advent of the Socialists to power under Guy Mollet would lead to a revision of French policy on Algeria, but the Suez fiasco dashed any illusions he held on that score. What further embittered Fanon was the broad-based support voiced by the French public for intensifying the fight against the independence movement. In the spring of 1956 the French Socialist and Communist Parties—as well as the parties of the center and right—agreed to the imposition of "special powers" to crush the rebellion. Yet while the events in Algeria did not seem to cause any major crises or rethinking within the French left, matters were very different when it came to Hungary. Tens of thousands of communists in France and throughout Western Europe tore up their party cards and left their respective communist parties in response to the brutal Soviet repression of the workers' revolution in Budapest. Fanon, however, was not impressed. Why was so much being made of the Soviet suppression of Hungary when so little was said about France's suppression of Algeria? Fanon had been immersed in French society and culture for years, but his severe disappointment at the turn of events impacted him deeply, leading him to burn his bridges to France.

Fanon viewed Hungary 1956 as a decisive moment in the Cold War. But he never made a clear statement in support of the Hungarian revolution.[20] This is unfortunate: Hungary 1956 marked a decisive divide not between the superpowers but rather *within* the so-called "socialist" regimes. For the first time a full-fledged workers' revolution arose *against* a putatively "Soviet" state—a revolution that embraced the banner of humanism. In many respects it marked the beginning of the end of Soviet totalitarianism—something would take another 35 years to achieve.[21] While Fanon's disappointment with the French Left's refusal to take a stand in support of Algeria was commendable, his failure to make a category of what Hungary 1956 signified would prove problematic—especially when it came to clearly expressing the *class* nature of the USSR and explicitly warning against the pitfalls of its version of "socialism."

In Algeria itself, things were becoming increasingly precarious for Fanon. As the fighting escalated, so did the number of militants who arrived at the doors of Blida seeking treatment—or protection from arrest. Fanon treated not only revolutionaries, but also their tormentors. Several members of the French army and paramilitaries, including those who engaged in systematic torture of prisoners, came to Blida asking for treatment and Fanon placed them into therapy and assisted them. He later discussed several such cases in his published writings, in which he pointed out the ways in which racism dehumanizes its perpetrators as well as its victims.

By the end of 1956 his position at Blida was becoming increasingly untenable and he was undoubtedly being watched by the French secret police. He received death threats as well as heard of plans to arrest him. Frustrated at the difficulties of continuing to work in such an environment, he resigned his position. Although he made no effort to publicize his reason for leaving—to do so would have been suicidal—his letter of resignation is a manifesto unto itself:

> Although the objective conditions under which psychiatry is practiced in Algeria constituted a challenge to common sense, it appeared to me that an effort should be made to attenuate the viciousness of a system of which the doctrinal foundations are a daily defiance of an authentically human outlook.

> For nearly three years I have placed myself wholly at the service of this country and of the men who inhabit it. I have not spared either my efforts or my enthusiasm. There is not a parcel of activity that has not had as its objective the unanimously hoped for emergence of a better world.

> But what can a man's enthusiasm and devotion achieve if everyday reality is a tissue of lies, of cowardice, of contempt for man?[22]

With the FLN in Tunisia

Fanon was expelled from Algeria shortly after handing in his letter of resignation, in January 1957. He had a lot of company. The severity of France's repression during and after the battle of Algiers—which began in June 1956 and brought the war directly into the cities— forced much of the FLN leadership, including Abane, into exile. Most of them, as well as Fanon, went to Tunisia, where the FLN had its headquarters (Tunisia became independent in March 1956 and was a strong supporter of the Algerian independence movement). Before arriving there Fanon spent about a month in France, where he met with several FLN members active in the underground. He also got in touch with friends like Ayme and Guérin, who noted that Fanon was now totally devoted to the Algerian struggle and in full accord with the decisions of the Soummam Conference.[23] He also met with those (such as Jeanson) who were trying to organize opposition against the war, but Fanon was unimpressed with the effort. By this point, he was saying his *adieu* to France; this was his last trip to the country.

Fanon arrived in Tunis in March 1957. One of the first people he met with upon his arrival was Abane. Things were not going well for him. Abane was a major advocate within the FLN of the policy of urban warfare, but the failure of the battle of Algiers undermined his position. The military commanders also did not take kindly to his sharp criticisms of them. The former were now getting the upper hand, since many of the political leaders were in exile. Neither Abane nor Fanon were pleased that the military commanders were subverting the decisions of the Soummam Conference by asserting their priority over the political leadership. Abane was being marginalized, but he still had enough influence to see to it that Fanon was appointed director of the FLN's press service. Fanon grew even closer to Abane over the next eight months (Abane was also living in Tunis) and they often met to discuss the politics of the Algerian movement.

Fanon as Revolutionary Journalist

As part of his responsibilities with the press service Fanon began contributing to the FLN's publication, *El Moudjahid*. Fanon eagerly threw himself into the work, but it did not consume the bulk of his time. He was still engaged in a considerable amount of work as a psychiatrist. Most (although it appears not all) of his contributions to *El Moudjahid* were published in *Toward the African Revolution* after his death. It is very easy to read these short pieces out of context. First, all of Fanon's contributions were unsigned and came out of a collective discussion with the editors. They were not simply expressions of his personal point of view.[24] Second, they were written in response to the immediate events of the day and do not represent the final word on many issues. It should therefore not come as a surprise that Fanon would later revise or change some of the views expressed in the pieces in *El Moudjahid*. This is not to downplay the importance of his journalistic work, since it marked the first time that he stepped forward publicly as a spokesperson for the FLN.

El Moudjahid came out in Arabic and French editions; Fanon wrote for the latter. One of the first subjects he was assigned to write about was the French left—no doubt because he was known as having many contacts with it over the years. His articles contain a devastating critique of the left and the working class for failing to fulfill its historic mission. He writes, "The generalized and sometimes truly bloody enthusiasm that has marked the participation of French workers and peasants in the war against the Algerian people has shaken to its foundations the myth of an effective opposition between the people and the government."

He goes even further: "The war in Algeria is being waged conscientiously by all Frenchmen and the few criticisms expressed up to the present time by a few individuals mention only certain methods which 'are precipitating the loss of Algeria.'"[25] Fanon's comments exhibit a sense of betrayal, of loss—of France having turned its back on its own ideals, ones that he was once inspired by: "After the fruitful struggle it waged two centuries ago for the respect of individual liberties and the rights of man, it finds itself today unable to wage a similar battle for the rights of peoples."[26] So much is this the case, that

> In a colonial country, it used to be said, there is a community of interests between the colonized people and the working class of

the colonialist country. The history of wars of liberation waged by the colonized peoples is the history of the non-verification of this thesis.[27]

Who used to say this if not communists and socialists? Yet they betrayed this "community of interests" by not supporting the Algerian struggle. Fanon's rage at the *organized* left was surely justified, given its failure to take a firm position for Algerian independence. And that failure has deep roots. It goes back to the refusal of many nineteenth-century socialists to support struggles for self-determination in the non-Western world—despite Marx's support of them.[28] The problem became acute after Marx's death, in the reticence (and sometimes outright refusal) of sections of the Second International to take a firm stand against imperialism. In France this has an especially egregious history. In the early 1920s the PCF contravened Lenin's position by resisting admonitions from the Communist International that it support national liberation in the colonies.[29] Such shortcomings are also evident in the tone-deafness of many socialists and communists to matters of race and racism—displayed even by such great figures as Eugene V. Debs, who held that there is no race question outside of the class question.[30] And it continues to show itself today in the view of many Marxists, anarchists and independent leftists that struggles for national liberation are inherently reactionary or a diversion from the "real" fight.[31] That Fanon chose not to identify himself with any existing current of the radical left, Marxist or otherwise, long before he got to Algeria, indicates that he did not see any of them as speaking to his lived experience as a black person.[32]

No tendency of the left comes in for harsher treatment by Fanon than the PCF. He writes

> The Communist Left, for its part, while proclaiming the necessity for colonial countries to evolve toward independence, requires the maintenance of special links with France. Such positions clearly manifest that even the so-called extremist parties consider that France has rights in Algeria.[33]

He then states that the main problem with groups like the PCF is that they "do not always perceive the colonialist—or to use a new concept—the neocolonialist character of their attitude."[34] This essay of December 1957 is the first time that he uses the term "neocolonialism." It is often overlooked that Fanon first posits this new concept in taking issue with a part of the *left*. He did not view neocolonialism as purely a function of bourgeois society; he held that much of the left is invested in it as well.

To be sure, Fanon's articles in *El Moudjahid* critique the political parties of the *organized* left. He makes little or no mention of individual figures that did speak out against the war and the small but sometimes influential groupings that took a stand for Algerian independence— which the French right viewed as an act of treason. As early as 1955 *Les Tempes Modernes* (the journal edited by Sartre, Merleau-Ponty, and Simone de Beauvoir) published material supporting Algerian independence, and Jean-François Lyotard (himself from Algeria, as was Jacques Derrida) wrote several pieces in support of the struggle in the same year. That said, such expressions of support by French intellectuals for the Algerian cause was exceptional; figures such as Foucault remained silent on the issue throughout the 1950s and early 1960s. This was no small matter: Algeria was *the* defining issue in French society at the time. To remain silent on this matter was tantamount to moral and political abdication to existing society.

Fanon therefore had his reasons for burning his bridges to France. In his articles in *El Moudhajid*, he did not bother to mention the relatively few cases in which leftist intellectuals voiced opposition to the war. Given his many contacts in France, he could hardly have been unaware of such developments. His silence about them may have been a result of his role as a FLN spokesperson in working for *El Moudjahid*. The FLN, like any national liberation movement, would be primarily interested in whether it had support from political tendencies that were in the position to impact French policy, such as the major political parties of the left. Fanon was unable to detect any signs of support from that direction, and this largely explains the rather sweeping tone of his critique of the French political scene.

Fanon and the European Working Class

Nevertheless, the organized left is one thing; the working class as a whole is another. Was Fanon overstating matters in denying that there is *any* community of interests between the workers of the colonialist country and the "wretched of the earth" in the colonies? Based upon Fanon's own words the answer is *yes*. Only a year after dismissing the European working class, Fanon stated in another piece for *El Moudjahid*, "The dialectical strengthening that occurs between the movement of liberation of the colonized peoples and the emancipatory struggle of the exploited working class of the imperialist countries is sometimes neglected, and indeed forgotten."[35] Indeed, it appears it had been neglected and forgotten by himself! He now corrects this by speaking of "the internal relation . . . that unites the oppressed peoples to the exploited masses of the colonialist countries."[36]

This does not mean that Fanon became any less critical of the failure of the Western left to do what he expected of it when it came to Algeria. Nor did he start to look at the European working class through rose-colored glasses. Fanon was projecting a *hope*, an *expectation*, that the oppressed of the industrially developed world would one day rise to the challenge of reaching out to the anti-colonial struggles. He never closed the door to the possibility that the working class *might* fulfill its historic mission even while critiquing it for not yet having done so. As he wrote in *The Wretched of the Earth*

The colossal task, which consists of reintroducing man into the world, man in his totality, will be achieved with the crucial help of the European masses who would do well to confess that they have rallied behind the position of our common masters on colonial issues. In order to do this, the European masses must first of all decide to wake up, put on their thinking caps and stop playing the irresponsible game of Sleeping Beauty.[37]

The claim—voiced repeatedly over the years by rightists and leftists—that Fanon advocated a "Third World messianism" that ignored the revolutionary potential of the Western working class is patently false. Cornelius Castoriadis was especially off base in this regard: "Must we conclude that the only parties interested in revolution are African bushpeople and the living skeletons sleeping on the sidewalks of Calcutta? That is the conclusion drawn by another class of confusionists, like Fanon."[38]

Two Worlds in Algeria

Fanon also wrote a number of articles for *El Moudjahid* on the European minority in Algeria. His critique of French settlers in Algeria—which at the time constituted 10 percent of the populace—is harsh and biting:

> Every Frenchmen in Algeria is at the present time an enemy soldier. So long as Algeria is not independent, this logical consequence must be accepted . . . The Algerian experiences French colonialism as an undifferentiated whole, not out of simplemindedness or xenophobia but because in reality every Frenchmen in Algeria maintains, with reference to the Algerian, relations that are based on force.[39]

As with his comments on the Western working class, Fanon's statement that "every Frenchmen in Algeria oppresses, despises, dominates"[40] has often been taken out of context and read as if he was an atavistic nationalist who had come to hate all Europeans living in Algeria. This is not at all the case. Fanon wrote this in a specific political context—the FLN's escalation of attacks in urban areas during and after the battle of Algiers. He was seeking to explain why European civilians were often targeted. However, these early comments (made in 1957) on the French minority were not his last. Two years later he wrote very differently in *A Dying Colonialism*:

> We shall now show in detail that the European minority has in the past become diversified and that considerable numbers of non-Arab Algerians have identified themselves with the Algerian cause and collaborate actively in the struggle, while others officially fight in the ranks of the Algerian Revolution.[41]

As more Europeans broke from their privileged position and cast in their lot with the revolution, Fanon moved away from the sweeping and wholesale condemnation of them that characterized his earlier statements.

Moreover, when Fanon writes in *The Wretched of the Earth* of the "Manichaean" world in which the colonizer and colonist inhabit separate "zones" of being, he does not posit this as a dualism that is fixed and frozen for all time. He does not treat it as a Kantian antimony. He instead conceives of the national struggle as one that *breaks down* and *overcomes* this dualistic Manichaean world:

> The colonist is no longer simply public enemy number one. Some members of the colonialist population prove to be close, infinitely closer, to the nationalist struggle than certain native sons. The racial and racist dimension is transcended on both sides. Not every black or Muslim is automatically given a vote of confidence.[42]

As Sekyi-Otu insightfully puts it, "Fanon the narrator welcomes an end to the history of racist metaphysics of good and evil . . . Fanon's narrative rejoices, not this time in the death of the colonizer, but in the death of race as the principle of moral judgment."[43] The "death of race" is not achieved by a mere declaration, through a verbal swearing-off of racial privilege and "whiteness." It is achieved through an actual social transformation on the part of the oppressed in which the material and ideological powers responsible for our "Manichaean world" is thoroughly uprooted. Fanon does not let us forget that revolutions produce a fundamental transformation of the human personality—which can also extend to those who initially support the existing society. In doing so, revolutions point to the possibility of becoming liberated not only from racism but also from the concept of race itself.

Contradictions Within the Algerian Revolution

By 1958 Fanon had concluded that the Algerian revolution was not only important in its own right but the vanguard of the effort to liberate Africa as a whole. France preferred to hold onto its colonies, but by the late 1950s it realized that it was becoming increasingly difficult. In response, upon coming to power in 1958, De Gaulle began to promise a modicum of political independence to some of the French colonies in exchange for maintaining economic dominance over them through membership in the French Community. But Algeria was another matter. France would not let her go. Algeria was the strongest link in the chain of French imperialism. Fanon recognized that if the revolution in Algeria succeeded the entire neocolonial as well as colonial edifice of the continent would completely unravel. He argues his case as follows

> Many colonized peoples have demanded the end of colonialism, but rarely like the Algerian people. This refusal of progressive solutions, this contempt for the "stages" that break the revolutionary torrent and cause the people to unlearn the unshakeable will to take everything into their hands at once in order that everything may change, constitutes the fundamental characteristic of the struggle of the Algerian people.[44]

On these grounds Fanon placed greater emphasis on the difference between "the parliamentary phase" of anti-colonial struggle—in which non-violent means were used to secure independence—and the "armed struggle" which he saw as imperative in Algeria and elsewhere. Fanon was disappointed when many African countries voted in favor of De Gaulle's referendum to become part of the French Community, but he was thrilled when Sékou Touré of Guinea pushed for a No vote and opted for independence on its own terms. France was being forced out of sub-Sahara Africa, he stressed, because it was becoming so bogged down with the fighting in Algeria.[45] The future of Algeria, he held, would largely determine the future of Africa.

Things were not going that well, however, in Algeria itself. The years 1958 to 1960 proved one of the most difficult in the history of the struggle. France was committing massive military sources to the fight and the FLN often found itself on its heels. No less ominously, serious disputes had erupted within the FLN that were being "resolved" in very disturbing ways. Ahmed Ben Bella (who later became the first leader of independent Algeria in 1962–65) had long been an adversary of Abane's and opposed the Soummam Conference. But Abane had many other adversaries as well. By the summer of 1957 he was forced out of the FLN leadership, in part by

Abdelhafid Boussouf and Lakhdar Bentobbal. Fanon strongly disliked the latter two, telling a friend that they

> fail to envisage anything beyond independence and [are] constantly vying for power. Ask them what this future Algeria will look like, and they don't have a clue. The idea of a secular state or of socialism, the idea of man for that matter, these are things that are entirely alien to them . . . They want to have power in this new Algeria, but to what end? They themselves don't know. They think that anything that is not a simple truth is dangerous to the revolution.[46]

Fanon was concerned that conservative elements within the FLN that favored creating a society based on an Arab or Islamic identity were beginning to overshadow the more revolutionary elements of those like Abane. Fanon was never the slightest bit interested in either an Islamic state or defining the movement along Islamic lines—and not just because he was a confirmed atheist. He wanted the independence struggle to be a conduit to the creation of a new kind of person, a new humanity—not a reversion to tribal identities, traditional practices, and religious obscuranticism. Cherki reports that in this period

> Fanon worried about the shape of the new society that would emerge in post-Independence Algeria; the prospects were dim—a new bourgeoisie ready to pick up where the others had left off, or a power struggle between different clans, or a religious movement that would succeed in determining the nature of the State.[47]

Fanon became further disturbed when he learned that Abane—who he looked up to as the most farsighted leader in the FLN—was made to "disappear." He later learned that Abane's co-leaders murdered him. The circumstances of his death remained a secret; the FLN claimed he had died battling the French. Fanon knew better, but kept quiet about it. He felt that any open expression of disagreement would be used by the French to divide the movement, and he accepted the discipline that membership in a revolutionary organization engaged in armed struggle against a powerful enemy seemed to entail. He also knew that any public expression of disagreement could prove personally dangerous. There were reports—difficult to confirm—that Fanon's name was on a list of people to be "liquidated" if they reacted strongly to Abane's "disappearance."[48]

None of this altered Fanon's perspective on the vanguard role of the Algerian struggle. While he had differences with some in the leadership, there were many others among the rank-and-file as well as the leadership that he felt very close to and who shared many of his convictions and concerns. At the same time, Fanon's interests had grown beyond Algeria; he was becoming increasingly involved in the politics of sub-Saharan Africa. This would prove to be among his most important and enduring contributions to revolutionary theory and practice.

5

The Strategist of Revolution: Africa at the Crossroads

anon has often been heralded—or denounced—as a "theorist of Third World revolution," but the claim is somewhat misleading. He did not develop a universal theory of revolution applicable to every country in the developing world, and his comments on South or East Asia, the Middle East, and Latin America are rather sparse. From 1956 he was first and foremost an *Algerian* revolutionary who viewed its struggle as the critical determinant for the future of the *African* revolutions. He became intimately involved in the liberation movements in sub-Saharan Africa, but it was always as a representative of the FLN. This is not to say that Fanon's *ideas* do not speak to realities outside of Africa. There is every reason to consider him a *world* revolutionary. His writings on race, racism, and national culture at the end of his life—just like those at the beginning—have *global* ramifications, including for those living in the industrially developed West.

The Promotion of an African Legion

Fanon's first visit to sub-Saharan Africa was in December 1958, where he attended the All-African People's Congress in Accra, Ghana. It was called by Ghana's leader Kwame Nkrumah as a step to creating an independent United States of Africa. Ghana had taken the lead in becoming the first sub-Saharan African country to gain national independence (in 1957) and it was in the forefront of promoting Pan-Africanism. Fanon was part of a small FLN delegation but not its most senior member; he never became part of the FLN's ruling body. Fanon's brief speech largely consisted of a defense of the Algerian movement's use of armed struggle against French colonialism. He does not deny that independence could be achieved elsewhere through non-violent means (as was the case in Ghana). He states that the reason France has been forced to initiate a process of decolonization in sub-Saharan Africa is because of the pressure placed upon it by the armed struggle of the Algerians.

Fanon was especially concerned about the threat of neocolonialism: "The end of the colonial regime effected by peaceful means and made possible by the colonialist's understanding might under certain circumstances lead to a renewed collaboration of the two nations."[1] The more forceful the break between the former colony and the imperial power the less likely that the former would become sucked into the latter's orbit. This frames much of Fanon's later discussion of violence in *The Wretched of the Earth*. He also distinguishes between settler colonies (such as Algeria, Kenya, and South Africa) where violence is clearly needed, and other African colonies where it may not apply.

The most important point in his speech was the discussion of an African Legion to help liberate other parts of Africa. Several delegates discussed the idea, but Fanon was especially emphatic about it—as he was to be in many future conferences. He viewed the formation of an African Legion as a key determinant in the liberation of the continent and would never let go of stressing its importance.

Fanon's speech was well received, but it must have come out of the blue to some of the delegates—especially to Senghor, who was more interested in cementing ties with France than worrying about how to aid Algeria. Lip service to Pan-Africanism aside, many of the future leaders of the newly-independent-countries-to-be were more concerned about getting economic aid from Europe than pushing for a continental revolution. Yet many other African leaders that Fanon met and befriended for the first time at the conference held to a principled revolutionary position, such as Nkrumah, Patrice Lumumba of the Congo, Sékou Touré of Guinea, and Julius Nyerere of Tanzania (as well as Félix Moumié of Cameroon, whom he had known personally for some time).

The Rome Congress of 1959

At the end of March 1959 Fanon traveled to Rome to attend the Second Congress of Black Writers and Artists. He was not asked to speak as a representative of the Algerian movement. The conference was instead organized (by *Présence africaine*) around the theme of "the unity of Negro-African cultures." Fanon nevertheless staked out his own ground. His paper is an important turning point in his development, since it marks his decisive departure from negritude and wholesale embrace of the national liberation struggles as the conduit to a new humanism. He loudly proclaims

> The liberation struggle does not restore to national culture its former values and configurations. This struggle, which aims at a fundamental redistribution of relations between men, cannot leave intact either the form or substance of the people's culture. After the struggle is over, there is not only the demise of colonization, but also the demise of the colonized. This new humanity, for itself and for others, inevitably defines a new humanism. This new humanism is written into the objectives and methods of the struggle.[2]

This is quite a distance from negritude's effort to recapture an "authentic" black culture. The "demise of the colonized" signifies that the revolutionary subject is able to liberate itself from its former values and attachments. As against any ahistorical essentialism, he emphasizes the formation of new and unexpected cultural formations in and through the process of national liberation. As Fanon sees it

> There can be no such thing as rigorously identical cultures. To believe one can create a black culture is to forget oddly enough that "Negroes" are in the process of disappearing, since those who created them are witnessing the demise of their economic and cultural superiority. There will be no such thing as a black culture . . . [3]

Just as for Marx the ultimate aim of the proletarian revolution is not to elevate the proletariat as the ruling class but instead to abolish all classes and hence the proletariat itself, so for Fanon the ultimate aim of the national revolution is not to secure a home for blackness but to abolish the conditions of its very existence. *The death of race is indeed the goal of the national liberation struggle.* At the same time, this goal cannot be achieved by skipping over the particularity of racial identity and national demands. Fanon is absolutely emphatic on this point:

> And now the moment has come to denounce certain pharisees. Humanity, some say, has got past the stage of nationalist claims. The time has come to build larger political unions, and consequently the old-fashioned nationalists should correct their mistakes. We believe on the contrary that the mistake, heavy with consequences, would be to miss out on the national stage. If culture is the expression of the national consciousness, I shall have no hesitation in saying, in the case in point, that national consciousness is the highest form of culture.[4]

The individual cannot make it to the universal without the particular. This Hegelian syllogism, as we have seen, is the central philosophical motif at work in *Black Skin, White Masks*. The same Hegelian conception now shows itself in his speech at the Rome conference in 1959. To reach a new humanity we must endure "the seriousness, the suffering, the patience, and the labor of the negative."[5] The negativity of the particular must be endured and experienced in order to make the transition from the individual to the universal. The dialectical structure of Fanon's argument remains what it was in 1952. What has changed in the 1959 speech is his conceptualization of what constitutes the particular. It is no longer a matter of "losing"[6] oneself in negritude; it is now a matter of losing oneself in the national liberation struggle. *Only through this odyssey can we find our way home.*

> If man is judged by his acts, then I would say that the most urgent thing today for the African intellectual is the building of his nation. If this act is true, i.e., if it expresses the manifest will of

the people, if it reflects the restlessness of the African peoples, then it will necessarily lead to the discovery and advancement of universalizing values ... It is at the heart of national consciousness that international consciousness establishes itself and thrives.[7]

Fanon is rejecting negritude as the mediating term in the dialectic, not because blackness is a minor term, but because negritude is an *abstract* mediator, a pretense of cultural unity that is *disengaged* from the specific locus of national struggles that generate cultural renewal. National revolution now serves as the mediation because it embodies a *human* agent, masses of people aspiring for self-determination. The negativity that resides in the debased and degraded colonized subject is far more capable shaking loose the chains that bind our humanity than any abstract discourse about "cultural unity" or identity. Fanon is situating the national struggle at the core of the dialectic because only a concrete *human agent* that is actually *fighting* for liberation can achieve the new humanism he has been reaching for since he first reached intellectual maturity. It is not the color or race of the subject that is of cardinal importance, but its *relationship* to history in the making—an ongoing *revolutionary* project. Hence

It is not enough to reunite with the people in a past where they no longer exist . . . When the colonized intellectual writing for his people uses the past he must do so with the intention of opening up the future, of spurring them to action and fostering hope. But in order to secure hope, in order to give it substance, he must take part in the action and commit himself body and soul to the national struggle.[8]

As in *Black Skin, White Masks*, Fanon does not overlook the importance of radical subjectivity having a *substantial* basis. In his Rome speech he is venturing into new ground in identifying that substance as *national culture*. Fanon is also as keenly attentive to the dialectic of self-consciousness as he was in his earlier work: "Self-awareness does not mean closing the door on communication. Philosophy teaches us on the contrary that it is its guarantee. National consciousness, which is not nationalism, is alone capable of giving us an international dimension."[9]

Ambivalence? Or Dialectical Contradiction?

Some commentators of Fanon's work have interpreted his move away from negritude as either suggesting that he came to agree with Sartre's position in *Black Orpheus* that is critiqued in *Black Skin, White Masks* or that he was at least ambivalent about the relation between the black struggle and movements for national self-determination that are not defined in exclusively racial terms. Irene Gendizer, for one, makes a persuasive case that Fanon's Rome speech of 1959 reiterates his earlier view that a common link exists between blacks only to the extent that colonialism treats blacks as an undifferentiated entity:

> The same line of argument that Fanon had developed in *Black Skin, White Masks* reappeared. The African sees himself as the colonizer saw him; undifferentiated, a representative of blackness, a brother to all other black people. There were no African peoples, no nations, only the unrelieved blackness of the natives.[10]

This is, of course, an illusion: There is no more a universal bond connecting all blacks around the world than there is one connecting all whites. However, Gendzier is not correct that in 1959 Fanon "was now closer to Sartre's position" than in 1952. To be sure, Fanon has moved away from his earlier enthusiasm for negritude. But he has not done so by positing the black struggle as a minor term in the dialectic that must give way to what Sartre called "the more concrete" or "universal" mediator of the class struggle. Instead, Fanon posits the struggles of the African colonized subject as the mediating term. Moreover, as we will see in chapter 6, Fanon did not think that the national revolution could be conceived of in terms of the traditional class struggle. Thanks in large part to his debt to phenomenology he never let go of his insistence on not skipping over the actual lived experience of the subject—in this case, the *black* subject in Africa and elsewhere involved in national liberation struggles.

Gendizer nevertheless contends, "Fanon's commitments revealed a contradiction in his position that he, in effect, never fully resolved, between the wholehearted endorsement of nationalism, and his hope that it would nevertheless produce a nation prepared to transcend its limitations of nationalism."[11] This is questionable, since in the Rome speech Fanon does not issue a "wholehearted endorsement of nationalism." He wholeheartedly endorses the struggle for national culture and national liberation, which is not reducible (at least in his eyes) to nationalism. Nor does it appear that in the Rome speech he "remains divided between the genuine commitment he had to the Algerian movement on the one hand, and the continuing concern he felt for the predicament of black men and black society."[12] Fanon plunged into the Algerian movement not because he moved away from concern for "the predicament of black men and black society" but because he viewed the Algerian struggle as the vanguard force in weakening French colonialism and leading to the liberation of black Africa. He did not embrace Algeria's fight because he became won over to Arab nationalism, but rather because he saw it as a catalyst to the liberation of Africa as a whole. From the start of his career he understood that "blackness" is a creation of colonialism and that embracing any ontology of "blackness" buys into the very logic of racism. To transcend the fixation associated with racism it is necessary to posit, *as an absolute*, a particularity that is not fixed or essentialist but which is the conduit to a new humanism. By the late 1950s Fanon had wagered that he found that in the national liberation movement.

Still, is there not a contradiction between supporting a national struggle, which clearly has a nationalist *component*, and seeking to achieve universal human emancipation, which transcends any form of nationalism? There certainly is a "contradiction" here but it is not one that is a mere product of Fanon's making. Nor is it a matter of him being "ambivalent" about his commitments. *Rather, the contradiction is endemic to the revolutionary process itself.* Any effort to achieve emancipation entails a development through contradiction—a development from posing particular demands and perspectives to reaching for universal human emancipation. As Marx once put it, "the transcendence of self-estrangement follows the same course as self-estrangement."[13] There is a tenuous, contradictory relationship between means and ends, and there is no guarantee that it will be successfully navigated—whether we are speaking in terms of struggles over race, class or gender. An automatic, predetermined teleology is out of the question here. It is not possible to reach the goal except by certain means, but there is no guarantee that the means will be universally recognized as but a step to something else. It is always possible to fall prey to *fixation*, even in the struggle to liberate oneself from it. This problematic defines the very project of emancipation. One can wish the contradiction away, but it will not disappear. One can seek to deny it by skipping over the particular in order to leap to the universal, or one can ignore the universal in favor of the particular. But in either case the contradiction is unresolved and remains to haunt us.

Fanon understood, as Antonio Gramsci did before him, that the serious revolutionary philosopher-activist neither denies the objectivity of contradiction nor stands outside of it. Gramsci wrote in his *Prison Notebooks*

> The philosophy of praxis is consciousness full of contradictions in which the philosopher himself, understood both individually and as an entire social group, not merely grasps the contradictions, but posits himself as an element of the contradictions and elevates this element to a principle of knowledge and therefore of action.[14]

A Dying Colonialism

A few months after the Rome conference, Fanon decided to set down his thoughts about the national liberation struggle in a new book. Published in English as *A Dying Colonialism*, its original title is *L'An Cinq de la Révolution Algérienne* (Year Five of the Algerian Revolution). Its aim is to "look more closely at the reality of Algeria. We must not simply fly over it. We must, on the contrary, walk step by step along the great wound inflicted on the Algerian soil and the Algerian people."[15]

The "great wound" has been that of a fierce, violent struggle. For the native Algerians, it has taken the form of severe attacks and torture by the colonial authorities. Fighting fire with fire will not heal this wound.

> The FLN, at the time when the people were undergoing the most massive assaults of colonialism, did not hesitate to prohibit certain forms of action and constantly to remind the fighting units of the international laws of war. In a war of liberation, the colonized people must win, but they must do so cleanly, without "barbarity."[16]

Use of torture against captured soldiers is ruled out, as is indiscriminate attacks against civilians. The violent repression of French troops and paramilitaries does not justify replicating their methods: "We condemn, with pain in our hearts, those brothers who have flung themselves into revolutionary action with the almost psychological brutality that centuries of oppression give rise to and feed."[17] Certain means must be ruled out ahead of time; otherwise, achieving the ultimate end of new human relations is compromised:

> The new relations are not the result of one barbarism replacing another barbarism, of one crushing of man replacing another crushing of man. What we Algerians want is to discover the man behind the colonizer; this man who is both the organizer and the victim of a system that has chocked him and reduced him to silence.[18]

These are not the words of someone who advocates the "metaphysics of violence." Nor are they the words of someone who endorses "revolutionary terror." Speaking of the *fidai*, the Muslim who commits to fighting onto death if necessary, he states:

> The "terrorist," from the moment he undertakes an assignment, allows death to enter into his soul. He has a rendezvous with death. The *fidai*, on the other hand, has a rendezvous with the life of the Revolution, and with his own life. The *fidai* is not one of the sacrificed. To be sure, he does not shrink before the possibility of losing his life or the independence of his country, but at no moment does he choose death.[19]

The aim of the book is not only to have us enter the great wound of Algeria, but for us to find in that zone of negativity the font of the positive—the emerging effort to transform social and personal relations through a revolution. The echo of Hegel's discussion in the *Phenomenology* is too apparent to be ignored: "But the life of Spirit is not the life that shrinks from death and keeps itself untouched by devastation, but rather the life that endures it and maintains itself in it. It wins its truth only when, in utter dismemberment, it finds itself."[20]

Algeria Unveiled

Fanon opens the book with a famous chapter entitled "Algeria Unveiled," which examines the transformation of gender relations in the revolutionary process. This is not the first time that Fanon has delved into the man/woman relationship. *Black Skin, White Masks* devoted two chapters to relations between the sexes. But there the focus was on how men and women are victims of an inferiority complex. Here the focus is on the overcoming of such complexes.

Fanon's chapter is one of the most widely discussed among his body of work, and as is the case with much of his legacy, his words are often taken out of context. This is largely due to his discussion of how the wearing of the veil by Muslim women becomes part of their effort to resist the modernizing tendencies of the colonial regime and conceal their identity as they heroically fight for the revolution:

> Removed and resumed again and again, the veil has been manipulated, transformed into a technique of camouflage, into a means of struggle . . . Spontaneously and without being told, the Algerian women who had long since dropped the veil once again donned the *haik*, thus affirming that it was not true that women liberated herself at the invitation of France . . . The veil was worn because tradition demanded a rigid separation of the sexes, but also because the occupier was bent on unveiling Algeria.[21]

Is not Fanon endorsing the wearing of the veil? Does he see in this traditional form of women's subjugation a sign of their liberation?

Is he falling victim to an atavistic traditionalism? Some have even tried to read into this a defense of Islamic fundamentalism. But Fanon is doing no such thing. He does not *endorse* the veil. He instead *describes* a response by Algerian women to colonial domination. He acknowledges that taking up the veil involves a *regression*:

> Colonialism wants everything to come of it. But the dominant psychological feature of the colonized is to withdraw before any invitation of the conqueror's. In organizing the famous cavalcade of May 13th,* colonialism has obliged Algerian society to go back to methods of struggle already outmoded. In a certain sense, the different ceremonies have caused a turning back, a regression.[22]

Colonial domination is so overpowering that the oppressed often respond by becoming reified into their forms of opposition. This is a form of *fixation*, but not one imposed by existing society; it arises from their response to it. But it is fixation all the same, and Fanon has always believed "There should be no attempt to fixate man, since it is his destiny to be unleashed."[23] He is therefore by no means uncritical of wearing the veil: "The doctrinal assertions of colonialism in its attempt to justify the maintenance of its domination almost always push the colonized to the position of making uncompromising, rigid, static counter-proposals."[24]

The colonized exists in negative self-relation to the colonizer. Its initial act of resistance is therefore dependent on the object of its critique. As Fanon put it earlier, "As long as he has not been effectively recognized by the Other, it is this Other who remains the focus of his actions."[25] The colonized woman confirms her non-recognition by the Other in making herself unrecognizable: "This woman who sees without being seen frustrates the colonizer. There is no reciprocity . . . He does not see her." The glance of the Other is blocked—there is a "disturbance to which the phenomenology of the encounters has accustomed us."[26] *But this is not the end of the matter.* This only

---

* This is a reference to the aborted coup attempt of May 13, 1958 by right-wing French officers attempting to force the French government to adopt even-harsher measures against the Algerian revolution.

corresponds to what Fanon calls the "first phase" of the struggle. In due course the negative self-relation to the Other is itself negated: "In a second phase, the mutation occurred in connection with the Revolution and under special circumstances. The veil was abandoned in the course of revolutionary action."[27]

Those who are not attuned to the philosophical structure of Fanon's arguments will probably not be able to make much sense of what he is saying. He is certainly not giving a blanket endorsement of traditional forms of social existence.

This becomes even more evident from his discussion of how the national liberation struggle is altering relations inside the family between men and women, and between parents and children. He says that women are now speaking up and challenging men, refusing to be restricted to the home by venturing out into political activity, and insisting that marriages no longer be arranged but become voluntary. Fanon is clearly not just describing but endorsing *these* changes. He writes

> All these restrictions were to be knocked over and challenged by the national liberation struggle. The unveiled Algerian woman, who had assumed an increasingly important place in revolutionary action, developed her personality, discovered the exalting realm of responsibility. The freedom of the Algerian people from then on became identified with women's liberation, with her entry into history.[28]

Fanon may well be exaggerating. If such widespread and fundamental changes as he describes took place, how does one explain the ease with which the male leaders of the FLN imposed a hierarchical, male-dominated system so soon after independence? If gender relations changed that much would we not expect a powerful push back on the part of Algerian women? Yet this does not appear to have been the case. Fanon acknowledges, "no revolution can, with finality and without repercussions, make a clean sweep of well-nigh instinctive modes of behavior."[29] Yet he can be accused of making claims that are difficult to empirically substantiate.

That said, Fanon is not writing an empirical study. He is not engaged in an exercise in radical sociology. He is instead trying to produce awareness of revolutionary possibilities. He is seeking to elicit the necessity that is concealed by the semblance of contingency. It is hard to argue for a new humanism unless the emergent possibilities of new beginnings are at least elucidated. There are worse crimes to be accused of than exaggeration. Cynical lack of sensitivity to the emergence of new possibilities is one of them, which our age has in surplus.

Language and Liberation

Fanon's disclosure of the revolutionary possibilities emerging from the Algerian revolution is even more poignantly captured in his discussion of the transformation of attitudes toward media and language. The radio, he shows, was for many years a tool of colonial domination and shunned by many Arabs and Kabyles who saw it as the voice of the colonizer. When the national liberation takes off, such attitudes are rapidly transformed. The masses now want to make contact with each other, get news of the ongoing struggle, and make their own voice heard as they feel increasingly emboldened by the fight. Faced with large-scale illiteracy (the French gave little attention to educating the Muslim populace), the masses turn to the radio—just when the liberation is intensifying, in 1956. Clandestine stations such as "The Voice of Fighting Algeria" take off and obtain a mass audience. Fanon's discussion makes for a fascinating read in light of how forms of social media have been spontaneously appropriated and utilized by numerous mass movements and social struggles in the decades since his death.

No less important is his discussion of the transformations in language. He notes that prior to 1954 most of the congresses of the Algerian national movement were held in Arabic. This was in part a reflection of the effort to resist French cultural imperialism and assert the dignity of the native Arab tongue. Yet it also meant that the Kabyle populace was put in the position of having to speak in Arabic in order to take part in the deliberations. Faced with the need to overcome such divisions, the resistance movement began to adopt a different attitude to the French language, seeing it as an instrument of their very liberation. Referring to the Soummam Conference, he writes:

> In August 1956, the reality of combat and the confusion of the occupier stripped the Arabic language of its sacred character, and the French language of its negative connotations. The new language of the nation could then make itself known through multiple meaningful channels.[30]

Fanon sees this as having *philosophical* significance. He states, "What is involved here is not the emergence of an ambivalence, but rather a mutation, a radical change of valence, not a back-and-forth movement but a dialectical progression."[31] Adopting the colonizer's language to serve revolutionary ends becomes a moment in the transformation of reality: "The nation's *speech*, the nation's spoken *words* shape the world while at the same time renewing it."[32] *Man's consciousness not only reflects the objective world, but creates it.*[33] Fanon's comments echo Raya Dunayevskaya's later statement that "thought molds the form of experience and 'the ways in which consciousness must know the object as itself.'"[34] Fanon is clearly writing in a very different vein than the vulgar materialism and positivism that dominated much of radical thought in the twentieth century.

Fanon concludes *A Dying Colonialism* stating, "We say firmly that Algerian man and Algerian society have stripped themselves of the mental sedimentation and of the emotional and intellectual handicaps which results from 130 years of oppression." Half a century earlier, Rosa Luxemburg wrote of the "mental sediment" left by the liberation struggles of the masses.[35] These form the humus, she argued, for future freedom struggles—even when those that gave birth to them have long vanished from conscious memory. Fanon writes very much in her spirit.

The Ambassador of Revolution

With *A Dying Colonialism* Fanon became increasingly recognized as an important revolutionary figure, both inside and outside Algeria. This did not escape the notice of the French secret police. During a trip to Morocco in June 1959 he was seriously injured in a car accident, suffering acute trauma to his vertebrae. It was widely assumed that the French were responsible. Any doubts on this score were dispelled when a car exploded that was scheduled to pick him up in Rome, where he went for treatment. He narrowly averted another attempt to have him killed in the hospital by secretly moving to a different room. Nevertheless, Fanon was in good enough condition by August to return to Tunis, where he took part in a series of meetings with the FLN. He was appointed to a commission to help draw up new statutes for the group, especially concerning its relationship with the peasantry. This seems to be the one time that he had direct input in the formation of FLN policy.[36]

The main arena of Fanon's political activity in this period was sub-Saharan Africa. The reason is simple: 1960 was the "year of Africa," when 17 African countries attained independence. There was much to do to make their independence sustainable and he visited many of the new states as well as others still trying to create one. This left Fanon with little time for psychiatry, which he hoped to return to at another time; he toyed with the idea of creating a mental health system for Africa after independence.[37] He also spent less time in Tunisia, and stopped writing for *El Moudjahid*.

In early 1960 the GPRA, the Algerian Provisional Government, made him its ambassador to sub-Saharan Africa.[38] This did not mean that he was now in the inner circle of the FLN. The post, while important for Fanon, was not the main priority for the organization. Fanon nevertheless made the best of the opportunity by traveling to Guinea, Ivory Coast, Mali, Congo, Ethiopia, and elsewhere. Ghana, where he was based, was one of several English-speaking countries that he visited. Most of his work in Accra centered on trying to get the African Legion off the ground. In January 1960 he spoke at a conference in Tunis, stating that the creation of such a force would be a beacon for all of Africa. In March he traveled to Cairo to get the FLN's endorsement of his efforts. The FLN agreed in principle, but it did not appear to view it as a major priority. Ghana and Guinea (as well as Liberia) were supportive of Fanon's efforts, though the number of resolutions calling for the Legion outweighed the resources put into creating one. Numerous trips followed: April 7–10, 1960 in Accra for the Conference on Peace and Security in Africa; April 12–15 in Conakry, Guinea for the Afro-Asian Solidarity Conference; late April 1960 in Accra for Conference on Positive Action; shortly afterward, a trip to Liberia. At the June 14–20, 1960 Conference of Independent African States in Addis Ababa, Ethiopia, Fanon's proposal for an African Legion was strongly endorsed, and Nkrumah set up several training centers in Ghana to get it started.

Fanon made all of these trips as part of his work as a representative of the GPRA. He was not moving away from his devotion to the Algerian cause; on the contrary, his diplomatic activities deepened it. One reason he was so insistent on the formation of an African Legion was that the fate of the Algerian revolution, he held, depended on obtaining aid and armed support from the rest of Africa.

Perhaps the most important trip was to Léopoldville (now Kinshasa) in late August 1960 for the Pan-African Congress, convened by Patrice Lumumba. Congo was at a critical crossroads. The *Force Publique* had mutinied, Katanga Province had seceded, and Lumumba's hold on power had become extremely precarious.[39] If there was any place that needed an African Legion, it was Congo. With the army in shambles, Katanga in rebellion, and the Belgians and Americans plotting his demise, Lumumba was in desperate straits. He responded by calling in UN troops, who promptly stabbed him in the back by defending Belgium's neocolonial interests. He then asked the Russians for assistance, which spelled his doom: Eisenhower sent out the word that he had to be gotten rid of. He was murdered on January 17, 1961.

Fanon was very close to Lumumba and considered him Africa's greatest independence leader. He was devastated by his death. The title of his obituary—"Lumumba's Death: Could We Do Otherwise?"—is a sigh of distress that more was not done to support him. The painful lesson of Lumumba, he writes, is that "if we need outside aid, less us call on our friends"—not the UN or the Russians.[40] But who could those "friends" have been if not Ghana's Nkrumah and Guinea's Touré? They were the most enthusiastic advocates of an African Legion. But when the moment of decision came for Congo, their help was nowhere to be found.

Fanon, for his part, had always viewed the African Legion largely in terms of aiding Algeria. It was, after all, in the midst of a brutal fight with the French and victory for the FLN was by no means a foregone conclusion in 1960. He had long argued that Algeria was the lynchpin of the African liberation movement. In his essay on Lumumba, however, he suggests that that role fell to the Congo:

> Lumumba had once proclaimed that the liberation of the Congo would be the first phase of the complete independence of Central and Southern Africa and he had set his next objectives very precisely: support of the nationalist movements in Rhodesia, in Angola, in South Africa. A unified Congo having as its head a militant anti-colonialist constituted a real danger for South Africa, that very deep South Africa before which the rest of the world veils its face.[41]

Since South Africa was the wealthiest country in Africa, it goes without saying that the defeat of South African apartheid would have transformed the face of the continent, dramatically changing the prospects for the African revolutions as a whole. Its liberation would deliver a serious blow to neocolonialism.

Nevertheless, Fanon wrote these words about the role of the Congo after Lumumba's demise. No African Legion came on the scene to save him. And much of the discussion of the need for the Legion had focused on Algeria. Yet was the FLN really that concerned about sub-Saharan Africa? It placed greater weight on its relations with Arab countries and the Middle East. Despite telling friends in Tunis "we should all go to Congo to help Lumumba,"[42] Fanon's focus on the priority of the Algerian movement did little to place support for Congo in the foreground. In this sense, he was somewhat led astray by his insistence on the vanguard role of the Algerian Revolution.

The Southern Front

Fanon never wavered from his view of the leading role of the Algerian struggle. Indeed, it appears to have intensified in the aftermath of Lumumba's death. Fanon was in fact deeply troubled by what was occurring in Algeria. He feared that the French would strike a rotten compromise with the FLN and keep Algeria in its neocolonial orbit, just as it had done with so many newly independent African countries. The only way to avoid that, he felt, was to provide the revolution with enough material support to maintain the armed struggle. But there was a problem. The French had built an electronic fence on the Algerian-Tunisian and Algerian-Moroccan border, making it difficult for the FLN to get arms and ammunition to the forces of the interior. The longer the situation persisted, the more likely that the FLN would be forced into an unprincipled settlement. What then to do? What was needed, Fanon decided, was to create a new front to convey arms and ammunition from West Africa to southern Algeria. He spent much of the rest of 1960 mapping out what become known as the "southern front" of the Algerian revolution.

Fanon secured funding and light arms from Ghana, as well as support from Guinea and Mali, and in September 1960 he set out from Kankan, Guinea to reconnoiter a route to southern Algeria. The revolutionary diplomat had become the navigator for the delivery of military weapons. With a small number of colleagues, he followed ancient trade routes through the Maghreb to map out the feasibility of the enterprise. During the long and difficult trip, he came across a collection of books in Kidal on the ancient empires of Mali, Ghana, and Gao and consumed them with a passion. This was not the act of a man smitten with negritude's fascination with ancient sources of African wisdom. He was now looking to the past in order to better navigate a path to support an ongoing revolution. The dialectics of revolution gave new meaning to the past, making it a moment of the present—and future. Fanon spelled out his aim as follows:

Our mission: to open the southern front. To transport arms and munitions from Bamako. Stir up the Saharan population, infiltrate to the Algerian high plateaus. After carrying Algeria to the four corners of Africa, move up with all Africa toward African Algeria, toward the North, the continental city. What I should like: great lines, great navigation channels through the desert. Subdue the desert, deny it, assemble Africa, create the continent.[43]

Fanon's journey was exhausting, but it was successful in showing that forging a route for sending arms from West Africa to southern Algeria could be done. He traveled over 1,200 miles in all, and returned to Ghana feeling he had made important progress. But there was a problem: Fanon was feeling seriously ill and was unable to perform his normal workload. In December 1960 he was diagnosed with myeloid leukemia, for which there was little treatment at the time. Faced with an early death, Fanon decided to devote his last months to one final philosophical work.

6

Toward a New Humanity: The Wretched of the Earth

anon was a consistent supporter of the Soummam Conference of 1956, which insisted on the priority of the political leadership over the military commanders and the forces of the interior over those of the exterior. In practice, the decisions made at Soummam were often ignored. FLN lenders tended to relegate political goals to military concerns and those who objected (like Abane) were pushed aside.[1] Fanon had been very close to Abane, but he was no longer on the scene by 1960 and a new objective situation had arisen. The issue now before the FLN was whether to enter into negotiations with the French, and on what terms. The GPRA favored direct negotiations, but Fanon was becoming increasingly skeptical about the outcome. He had already seen too many rotten compromises in sub-Saharan Africa.

In this period Fanon became close with Houari Boumédienne, who at the time was head of the Frontier Army (and later President of Algeria, from 1965 to 1978). Fanon's connection with him may be somewhat surprising, since Boumédienne had tended to assert the priority of the commanders over the political leadership and he was by no means the most radical figure within the FLN. Nevertheless, Fanon's "perception of the Frontier Army as the wellspring of renewed revolutionary zeal began to take hold . . . [their] self-acknowledged peasant backgrounds, seemed to resist the idea of settling for a fictitious independence of the neocolonial sort."[2] Fanon was trying to make connections with those who could push back against any hasty compromise with the French, and the armed peasant fighters in the Frontier Army seemed to him one of the few sources that could be relied upon. All the same, he was disturbed by the hierarchical structure and lack of freedom of speech that he found in the army.

Boumédienne nevertheless invited Fanon to give a series of lectures to his troops at Ghardimaou, just inside the Tunisian border with Algeria. The content of Fanon's lectures remains unknown, but it is likely that they consisted of material he was preparing for *The Wretched of the Earth*.[3] It is crucial to keep in mind this political context in which the book was formed. Otherwise, much of what it says about violence, the role of the peasantry, and the threats facing the liberation movements from a new bureaucracy can be easily misconstrued.

There is also the personal context to consider. Fanon was slowly dying, and he knew that time was running out. He was sent to the USSR for medical treatment in January 1961 (it had an unwarranted reputation at the time for having an advanced medical system), but Fanon's illness persisted. Returning to Tunisia, he wrote the book quickly, within a few months. During this period he went to Rome to meet with Sartre and De Beauvoir. It was their first personal encounter. Sartre had by now come out strongly in support of the Algerian revolution and Fanon was very impressed with his *Critique of Dialectical Reason*, which attempted to forge a bridge between existentialism and Marxism. They were involved in deep discussions lasting days at a time, and Fanon asked Sartre to write the Preface to *The Wretched of the Earth*. One chapter of it was published in *Les Tempes Modernes* in May 1961.

Fanon's Warning

The Wretched of the Earth, which was Fanon's political, intellectual and personal testament, has become renowned for its prescient warning of the dead-ends and regression that would afflict so many newly-independent countries in the developing world. Composed just when many African nations had finally won their freedom from colonialism and as Algeria was poised to do the same, the book eschews any celebratory mode. It instead issues a dire prognosis of what is to come. It laments the fact that "for 95 per cent of the population in the developing countries, independence has not brought any immediate change. Any observer with a keen eye is aware of a kind of latent discontent which like glowing embers constantly threatens to flare up again."[4] He goes so far as to write: "It will be clear to everyone that no progress has been made since independence and that everything has to be started over again from scratch."[5] Deeply disturbed by growing conflicts between African states, the influence of regionalism and tribalism, and the rise of Islamic religious fanaticism,[6] he bemoans the fact that "we have switched from nationalism to ultranationalism, chauvinism, and racism."[7]

One can therefore be excused for experiencing a sort of cognitive dissonance in reading its opening pages, as Fanon declares that "the social fabric has been changed inside and out" by the national liberation movements.[8] He writes

> Decolonization never goes unnoticed, for it focuses on and fundamentally alters being, and transforms the spectator crushed to a nonessential state into a privileged actor, captured in a virtually grandiose fashion by the spotlight of History. It infuses a new rhythm, specific to a new generation of men, with a new language and a new humanity. Decolonization is truly the creation of new men. The "thing" colonized becomes a man through the very process of liberation.[9]

How can "no progress" be made since independence when the struggle to achieve it has "fundamentally altered being"? Are we simply being treated here to an exercise in rhetorical excess? Fanon is actually proceeding quite deliberately. His aim is to dissect the tragic outcome of the revolutions—those that have occurred and those still on the horizon. At the same time, he is aware that their outcome threatens to subsume recognition of what has been gained through the struggle. The process gets lost in the product, especially when aborted or unfinished revolutions occur. Are we not ourselves a tragic witness to this, given how the very memory of what was achieved in the African revolutions has almost entirely receded from view? Fanon begins by bracketing out the outcome in order to first bring into view the creative energies and accomplishments of the masses. They are the ones who propelled the independence movement; they are the ones who "stormed the heavens"—and in the process, overcame their sense of inferiority in the face of the colonial oppressor. A new vision of emancipation was born from the struggle, a sense that some of the most impoverished and downtrodden people in the world could stand up to a major industrial and colonial power—and win. Fanon is by no means exaggerating in stressing the subjective transformations occurring during the revolutionary process. As one historian of the Algerian revolution argues

> To argue that the anticolonial struggle did not produce a revolution in Algeria is to ignore the substantive socioeconomic changes that occurred from that struggle. The most critical changes were the reversals in social and economic relations caused by the FLN's mobilization and control of the Muslim population in the early years; the rise to power, through the ANP or FLN, of Algerians from peasant backgrounds; the changes in property ownership following the exodus of the French; and the new sense of self-esteem and positive identity among independent Algerians, i.e., a psychological transformation that Fanon regards as indispensable to revolution.[10]

Fanon is of course writing prior to the point of independence being reached in Algeria. He is oppressively aware of the dangers facing the revolution, and pointing to its positive features in no way minimizes this. On the contrary, he proceeds as he does in the opening pages of the book in order to provide the subjective standpoint by which the revolution—in Algeria as well as elsewhere—can be *measured*. The presentation of the positive content of the freedom struggle provides the ground for grasping both the limitations of the revolution's results as well as what is needed to surmount them. Fanon is not only analyzing the present but writing a kind of letter to the future, insofar as he wants us to become aware of the revolutionary possibilities that are so often obscured.

So what does he tell us about the final result? We learn that the newly independent states become sucked into the world market and fall prey to neocolonial domination. No sooner do they achieve political independence than what becomes manifest is their economic dependence. The old colonial powers as well as the superpowers step in to direct the affairs of the newly born nation. Independence turns out to be "an empty, fragile shell."[11] Unable to provide the masses with the benefits that they expected from the struggle, the newly anointed leaders turn upon them and impose hierarchical social control— often at the point of a gun. "Neocolonialism, this portrait suggests, is not simply a surreptitious recapture of national resources by external agents in the aftermath of flag independence. Neocolonialism is an internal state of affairs, the unmasked recolonization of human existence by the blackest of skins."[12]

Here we have the limitations of the national bourgeoisie on full display. The African national bourgeoisie, like any bourgeoisie, wants to control the economy. However, unlike in the West, where the bourgeoisie came to political power through its control of productive resources, in Africa the colonial authorities denied the native bourgeoisie any such control. The native bourgeoisie therefore focuses on the kind of power that is more readily in reach—*political* power. It has no experience running an economy. Upon independence it still lacks economic power. It compensates for this by proclaiming the need for "nationalization" of industry.

> In its thinking, to nationalize does not mean placing the entire economy at the service of the nation, or satisfying all its requirements. To nationalize does not mean organizing the state on the basis of a new program of social relations. For the bourgeoisie, nationalization signifies very precisely the transfer into indigenous hands of privileges inherited from the colonial past.[13]

This is most clearly seen in the actions of despots like Mobutu, who at least through the 1970s made sure that a higher percentage of the Congo's economy was state-owned than anywhere else in Africa. Which did not stop him, of course, from helping to murder Patrice Lumumba and become a lackey of the U.S. Innumerable other examples abound, including Senghor's less repressive policies in Senegal.

At the same time, it takes no stretch of the imagination to realize that the drive to compensate for its economic weakness also explains why many members of the national bourgeoisie proclaim themselves to be "socialists." They are driven to compensate for their economic impotence by gaining control of the economy through the mechanism of the state. And they readily accepted "advice" from the putatively "socialist" regimes in the USSR and China to help them successfully manage this. "Socialist" ideology served (and to some degree, continues to do so in some cases) as a convenient foil to distract attention from the rulers' rapacious appetites as well as the growing chasm between them and the masses. Although Fanon does not mention by name such leaders as Nkrumah of Ghana and Touré of Guinea—no doubt because he still considers them important allies in the battle against Western imperialism—the *logic* of his analysis perfectly captures the dynamic of their political rule, economic policies, and social ideology. After Fanon's death, this will become far more evident.

Fanon had addressed the shortcomings of the national bourgeoisie even before writing *The Wretched of the Earth*. A year earlier he states

> In reality the colonized states that have reached independence by the political path seem to have no other concern than to find themselves a real battlefield with wounds and destruction. It is clear, however, that this psychological explanation, which appeals to a hypothetical need for release of pent-up aggressiveness, does not satisfy us. We must once again come back to the Marxist formula. The triumphant middle classes* are the most impetuous, the most enterprising, the most annexationist in the world.[14]

In *The Wretched of the Earth* his criticism of the shortcomings of the bourgeois stage of development become even more virulent:

> As we have seen, the inadequacies of the bourgeoisie are not restricted to economics. Achieving power in the name of a narrow-minded nationalism, in the name of race, and in spite of

---

*   By "middle class" Fanon is not referring to the middle-income sector of the working class (as the term is widely used today), but rather to the national bourgeoisie—that is, the professional and business class.

the magnificently worded declarations totally void of content, irresponsibly wielding phrases straight out of Europe's treatises on ethics and political philosophy, the bourgeoisie proves itself incapable of implementing a program with even a minimum of humanist content.[15]

What then, according to Fanon, is to be done? He says that where these conditions prevail the bourgeois stage should be *skipped*: "In the underdeveloped countries a bourgeois phase is out of the question. A police dictatorship or a caste of profiteers may very well be the case but a bourgeois society is doomed to failure."[16] He continues, "In the underdeveloped countries the bourgeoisie should not find conditions conducive to its existence and fulfillment."[17] This is a very radical position. It is not one that was put forth by any of the political tendencies leading the African revolutions, *including in Algeria.* The position held by the leaders of the anti-colonial movements, including the most radical of them, was that "national unity" precludes any perspective of putting aside the national bourgeoisie. Fanon is invoking an issue that Marxists had argued about for a half a century previously—that is, ever since the debates in the Second International on whether it is possible for developing societies to bypass a bourgeois stage of development.[18] This was also central to the discussions at Congress of the Communist International in Baku in 1920.[19] Fanon refers to this in writing:

The theoretical question, which has been posed for the last 50 years when addressing the history of the underdeveloped countries, i.e., whether the bourgeois phase can be effectively skipped, must be resolved through revolutionary action and not through reasoning. The bourgeois phase in the underdeveloped countries is only justified if the national bourgeoisie is sufficiently powerful, economically and technically, to build a bourgeois society, to create the conditions for a sizeable proletariat, to mechanize agriculture, and finally pave the way for a genuine national culture.[20]

Of course, Fanon has already shown that these conditions do not prevail in Africa, so the bourgeois phase, by his reasoning, cannot be "justified" there.

How then does Fanon envision "skipping" or surmounting the bourgeois stage of development? How does he envision overcoming the stalemate and outright regression that he sees as prevailing in the newly independent states—as well as those still struggling for independence?

The Dualities of Violence

Fanon's effort to find a pathway beyond the compromises and regression facing the newly independent states informs much of the first chapter of *The Wretched of the Earth*, "On Violence." Many have attacked his discussion for eulogizing violence as an end-in-itself, while others have defended it on the grounds that it simply defends the right of victims of violence to respond to it in kind. Neither view is accurate.

Fanon repeatedly stresses that violence is the organizing principle of the "Manichaean" world of colonialism. It exists in open, explicit forms as well as subtle and hidden ones, but in either case it is the central vehicle of racial and colonial domination. But Fanon surely knew this long before he wrote *The Wretched of the Earth*. So why does he enter into an extensive discussion of violence only in this book? It can hardly be due to the impact of Hegel's discussion of the violent "struggle unto death" for recognition in his *Phenomenology of Spirit*. After all, Fanon discusses that section of Hegel in *Black Skin, White Masks*—and yet the latter contains barely a word about violence. Nor do his various writings between 1952 and 1960 contain an extensive discussion of violence. Far more concrete considerations explain his focus on violence in *The Wretched of the Earth*—namely, the specific political situation facing him in 1961. The leaders of many African independence movements were making unprincipled compromises with the colonial powers, undoing many of the gains sought by the masses. Fanon feared that this pattern would repeat itself elsewhere— including in Algeria. How then could the self-activity of the masses be furthered instead of forestalled? Fanon decides that spelling out the positive features of violence could help encourage the masses not to accept rotten compromises from above but instead trust in their own initiatives. "Peaceful accommodation" was the last thing needed in the face of the machinations of neocolonialism and the treachery of the national bourgeoisie.

Colonialism, which shapes the colonized subject, is violent through and through. *Its very being is violence.* The being of the subject is itself *constituted* by violence. To ask the colonized to forgo violence without forgoing the violence of the colonial world is a contradiction in terms. For this reason he writes, "As soon as you and your fellow men are cut down like dogs there is no other solution but to use every means available to reestablish your weight as a human being."[21]

Fanon acknowledges that this can prove counter-productive, by leading the colonized subjects to turn on themselves. He writes, "Whereas the colonialist or police officer can beat the colonized subject day in and day out, insult him and shove him to his knees, it is not uncommon to see the colonized subject draw his knife at the slightest hostile or aggressive look from another colonized subject."[22] He does not eulogize violence as such. What he eulogizes is violence that is turned outward, against colonial and racist authority, in such a way that any unprincipled accommodation with it is foreclosed. Obviously, this represents a challenge not just to the colonizers but also to the nationalist leaders trying to cut a deal with them.

The notion that Fanon is fetishizing or glorifying violence *per se* makes sense only if we abstract from the specific political problem he is grappling with—how to ensure that the revolutions not remain confined within the limitations set by neocolonialism and the national bourgeoisie. But does violence really ensure the overcoming of these limits? David Macey makes a compelling case in arguing

In retrospect, it is hardly possible to claim that it is the absence of adequate illumination by violence that is responsible for the political tragedies of post-independence nations. It is the prohibition of politics and inadequacy of political organization that has robbed yesterday's partisans of their rewards.[23]

In certainly appears that this judgment is confirmed by the outcome of many African revolutions that *did* employ violence—such as in Angola. Fanon supported the wing of the Angolan independence movement that was initially most receptive to taking up arms and waging an extensive guerrilla war, Holden Roberto's Union of the Peoples of Angola (UPA). Yet it ended up allying itself with the CIA in opposition to the more progressive tendencies in the revolution. Even if we disregard Roberto, the UPA contained a host of shady characters. Jonas Savimbi, who was later to wreak so much violence and destruction upon independent Angola, was at the time a member of the UPA (he left it to form UNITA in 1966, with assistance from the Chinese government). He subsequently waged a three-decade-long war against the more-progressive MPLA.

Although Fanon did not single out violence for "metaphysical" reasons but in regard to a specific political problematic facing him at the time, most of his biographers acknowledge that it led him to some mistaken judgments. Peter Geismar argues

> Fanon turned toward the nationalist army as another source of revolutionary momentum. He had more faith in the men using the guns than those arranging the peace; warriors, hardened to violence, would be less tolerant of neocolonialist enterprises . . . His greatest concern, by 1961, was that a Moslem bourgeoisie would replace the European settlers without any real restructuring of Algerian society. He had a naïve belief that the army would supervise the growth of Third World socialism, remaining immune from the materialistic corruptions of the new bourgeoisie.[24]

Fanon gives such weight to violence, however, for an additional (albeit related) reason: he sees it as a means by which the colonized can overcome their inferiority complex. Fanon's response to reading Engels's discussion of violence in *Anti-Dühring* (he was given a copy by Rheda Malek, a philosophy student) illustrates his view of this. He was disappointed with Engels's discussion. This is not because Engels shied away from endorsing violence. On the contrary, it is a staple of Marxist theory that eliminating the property-right of the bourgeoisie over the means of production will evoke a violent reaction that a revolution must arm itself against (the case of the American Civil War, when the Confederacy took up arms to defend the master's property right over their slaves, indicates just how violent that response can be—even when the existence of private ownership of the means of production and wage labor is not called into question). Nor did Fanon differ from Engels when it came to understanding that no revolution could be successful unless the revolutionaries obtain a monopoly on the exercise of armed force (a revolutionary government that comes to power with the military still under the control of the old ruling classes is a recipe for disaster). Rather, Fanon was dissatisfied with Engels's discussion because he felt it was "too removed from the individual's qualitative experience of violence."[25] As he puts it in *The Wretched of the Earth*, "At the individual level, violence is a cleansing force. It rids the colonized of their inferiority complex, of their passive and despairing attitude. It emboldens them, and restores their self-confidence."[26]

There is something to be said for this. Taking it on the chin is not always the best way to gain subjective self-certainty, especially when living in conditions of continuous degradation. Fanon is not concerned with violence *per se* but rather the subjective transformation of the oppressed as a result of taking part in it. Violence is the predicate, not the subject, of his analysis. He emphasizes violence on the grounds that, in his view, it helps lift up and embolden the colonized subject. But is this rather sweeping declaration born out by evidence? It appears that the answer is in the negative. Recent studies, such as by Marnia Lazreg, which is based on extensive interviews with former FLN militants and others, indicates that violence has, at best, an ephemeral "cleansing" role. More often it dehumanizes and produces long-term distress in its participants. As Lazreg shows, "The temporary release that may be achieved through violence, and its long term transformative impact" are two very different things.[27]

For all the immense amount of attention given to what Fanon has to say about violence, it is not the strongest part of his analysis. If his effort to conceptualize the overcoming of the pitfalls facing the national liberation movements rested on his discussion of violence alone, it would hardly be satisfactory. Fortunately, that is not the case. Violence is only the initial and by no means the most important aspect of his discussion of how to overcome the entrapment of the revolution by the national bourgeoisie. This can hardly be seen, of course, if one does not read past the first chapter of the book—as many critics as well as supporters of Fanon seem to do.

The Peasantry and the Working Class

Far more important in Fanon's work is his discussion of the forces of revolution that can help the African revolutions continue in permanence. Central to this is the peasantry. The peasants tend to be neglected by the national bourgeoisie, which is based in the cities. The peasants constitute the majority of the populace, vastly outnumbering the working class and petty-bourgeoisie. Although they are not included in the agenda of the nationalist parties, they turn out to be the most revolutionary. Fanon loudly proclaims, "But it is obvious that in the colonial countries only the peasantry is revolutionary."[28] This is because of the specific form of social relations found in much of Africa. Since it has not undergone capitalistic indus-trialization on a large scale the working class is not a cohesive and compact force. It has not been *socialized* by the concentration and centralization of capital. The working class is dispersed, divided, and relatively weak. The peasantry, on the other hand, is socialized and relatively strong precisely because it has been left untouched by capitalist development. Their traditional communal traditions and social relations remain largely intact. They think and act like a cohesive group. They *live* the Manichaean divide that separates them from the colonizer. Therefore, the message of the revolution "always finds a response among the peasantry."[29]

The peasantry was not some distant abstraction to Fanon. He established direct contact with peasants even before he became an active revolutionary. Shortly after arriving at Blida he visited rural areas to better understand the indigenous peoples' understanding of madness. After he became a revolutionary he traveled many times to the countryside. And as noted earlier, he was involved in teaching the peasant recruits in the Frontier Army while at Ghardimaou. Fanon's discussion of the role of the peasantry is a theoretical generalization that is connected to first-hand experience—something that could not as readily be said of his writings on violence.

Fanon is looking to the peasantry as the revolutionary force that could be relied upon to take the revolution beyond the confines of the national bourgeoisie, since they never identified with it in the first place. The nationalist leaders keep their distance from them, hidden behind the curtain of urban existence. The working class, on the other hand, has tended to see the national bourgeoisie as a natural ally in its fight against colonial domination in the cities. This does not mean that Fanon ignores the role of the working class *tout court*. He supported the effort to establish an All-African Federation of Trade Unions and acknowledges the role of unions and other forms of working class organization in the struggle for independence. However, "since they never bothered to establish working links between their organization and the peasantry, who represent the only spontaneously revolutionary force in the country, the unions prove to be ineffective and realize the anachronistic nature of their program."[30]

Since the national bourgeoisie has little contact with the peasants before independence, they tend to have even less after independence. They wall themselves off in the cities and look abroad for aid and assistance—not to their own impoverished rural masses. The divide between the national bourgeoisie and the peasants becomes deeper. The peasants, however, have been socialized not only by their traditional communal formations but also by the revolutionary process. In many cases they constitute the bulk of the forces that fought colonialism. They have tasted battle, and are in no mood to be forgotten. They want to make their presence felt. Fanon is not simply positing the peasantry as the force behind the independence struggle but also as the catalyst to continue the revolution beyond it.

This does not mean that he is uncritical of the peasantry. He refers to "the obscuranticist tendencies of the rural masses" and warns that at times they exhibit a "reactionary, heated and spontaneous nature."[31] He is even more critical of the lumpenproletariat, citing its "lack of political consciousness and ignorance"[32]—even as he singles out its revolutionary role. He is aware that these forces can be manipulated in a non-revolutionary direction. His point is that this is only made all the easier when the revolutionary movement does not put down roots among them.

Re-Creating the Revolutionary Dialectic

Fanon is clearly challenging the standard Marxist model in posing the peasantry instead of the working class as the subject of revolution. He is not imposing a model that is adequate to Europe or the industrially developed West upon Africa, but focusing on the latter's specific social relations. He is especially attuned to how the additive of color impacts and transforms class relations in the colonial context. To simply apply a model of class relations developed in lieu of issues of race and racism onto a colonial context defined by racism makes no sense to him.

On can argue that it makes no sense in a *Marxian* understanding either. Marx held that in Western Europe the process of capitalistic development tears peasants from the "natural workshop" of the land; it *de-socializes* them and weakens them as a cohesive political force. This very process creates the urban proletariat, which is brought together by the concentration and centralization of capital to form a compact mass. It emerges as a cohesive political force through the socialization of labor. Marx did not pose the proletariat as the "universal class" because it was the most materially impoverished part of society. He well knew that the peasants are often much more impoverished. He did so because the working class possesses the ability to *totally* transform society because of its central place in the social relations of production. However, Marx did not claim that this process—traced out in Volume One of *Capital*—represents the inevitable course of development for the entire world. In the last decade of his life he affirms that societies experiencing different social conditions—in which the working class is a small part of the population and the peasantry has not yet been displaced from its traditional communal forms—could achieve a social revolution *ahead* of the West. The country he then had in mind was Russia, where 90 percent of the populace consisted of peasants.[33]

Most important of all, Marx insists throughout his work that a social revolution can be successful only if it is the product of "the self-conscious, independent movement of the immense majority, in the interest of the immense majority."[34] The notion that a socialist society could be created through the actions of a minority of the populace was completely anathema to Marx. His vision of socialist revolution was thoroughly *democratic* (obviously, this perspective did not inform the views of most of his self-proclaimed followers). Fanon's vision of emancipation is no less democratic, as seen in his insistence that the African revolutions could be successful only if they were rooted in the self-activity of the majority of the populace—who were clearly *peasants*.

In this sense, it can be argued that Fanon's discussion of the peasantry is in the spirit of Marx, even as it differs from his conclusions insofar as they pertain to Western Europe. "Marxism" is not a series of fixed conclusions that is applied willy-nilly to any and all realities regardless of their specific social content. Such an approach smacks of idealism, whereas Marx's approach is *historically materialist*. There is, however a great deal of idealism in formulaic and rigid variants of Marxism. Indeed, the reason that many orthodox Marxists wrongly take Fanon's comments about the leading revolutionary role of the peasantry *in Africa* as a generalization applicable to the entire world is that they themselves pay little heed to historical contingency and local realities in stressing "the leading role" of the working class.[35] Their standpoint is far more metaphysical than Fanon's. As Antonio Gramsci noted in his critique of Nikolai Bukharin (whom he viewed as an exemplar of vulgar Marxism), the latter failed to see his idealist shortcomings because to him "metaphysics means only a specific philosophical formulation, that of speculative idealism, rather than any systematic formulation that is put forward as an extra-historical truth, as an abstract universal outside of time and space."[36] In total contrast, by taking account of the fact that the African temporal and spatial context is radically different from that of Western Europe, Fanon adopts the same methodological approach as Marx insofar as he singles out the revolutionary role of specific social forces and their consciousness in strict relation to the nature of objective, material conditions.

Fanon's approach is therefore very distant from Trotskyism, which denies an *independent* political role to the peasantry. It is also very distant from Maoism, which heralds the peasantry as the universal class *in place of* the working class. Fanon makes no such claim. He does not say the peasantry is the primary subject of revolution in the entire world or even in the developing world. He says it is the primary subject in *Africa* at the time he is writing. Fanon's approach is always *phenomenological*, even in discussing the most immediate political realities.

Fanon's discussion of the role of the working class and peasantry can be questioned in terms of its applicability to all of Africa. His comment that the working class is the "bourgeois faction of the colonized population"[37] does not take into account the critical role played by the labor movement in Nigeria's fight for independence, when a series of strikes helped unify the nation across tribal lines for one of the few times in its history. It also does not take account of the labor movement in South Africa, which was to prove so instrumental in the dismantling of apartheid. Fanon's text is surely not the final word on these issues. His words live on, however, because the most important part of his discussion of the peasantry and working class concerns his repudiation of the two-stage theory of revolution in looking beyond the bourgeois phase of development. And it is precisely this that helps explain why he is so widely read in South Africa today, where a new generation is striving to go beyond the nationalist-bourgeois dominance of the African National Congress—a formation that has so clearly betrayed the hopes of the anti-apartheid activists who aimed for a fundamental transformation of social existence.[38]

Forms of Political and Social Organization

The most important dimension of Fanon's effort to discern an alternative course of development for the national liberation movements is his critique of the single-party state and advocacy of decentralized forms of political and social organization. Faced with severe economic problems and increasingly divorced from the masses, the national bourgeoisie embraces the elitist concept of a single "party to lead." It tries to compensate for its lack of serenity in economic matters by finding it in politics. Those who are not with it are now against it. He writes, "The single party is the modern form of the bourgeois dictatorship—stripped of mask, makeup, and scruples, cynical in every respect."[39] Fanon is ruthless in his critique: "The organic party, designed to enable the free circulation of an ideology based on the actual needs of the masses, has been transformed into a syndication of individual interests."[40] He argues

> In order to avoid these many pitfalls a persistent battle has to be waged to prevent the party from becoming a compliant instrument in the hands of a leader. Leader comes from the English verb "to lead," meaning "to drive" in French. The driver of people no longer exists today. People are no longer a herd and do not need to be driven . . . The nation should not be an affair run by a big boss.[41]

The single party initially arose to unify the country across tribal and ethnic lines, but over time it is not the people who runs the party, but the party that runs the people. Brilliantly anticipating later developments (as well as summing up many already in the making), he says the party evolves into little more than an "intelligence service" that spies on the masses and represses them. Opposition parties are brought to heel or are driven underground.[42]

This does not mean that Fanon rejects the need for a party. He wants a party that expresses the will of the masses, is free "of the very Western, very bourgeois, and hence very disparaging, idea that the masses are incapable of governing themselves." One of the great advantages of the nationalist parties is that they put the intellectuals in touch with the masses, enabling them to "witness the awakening of their intelligence and the development of their consciousness."[43] But that has now receded from view. The nationalist leadership now proclaims that the vehicle of "science" is the *bourgeois* intelligentsia.

Fanon wants to sweep aside the very idea of the single-party state, which requires that we "decentralize to the utmost."[44] He argues that nationalization of resources "must not take on the aspect of rigid state control." The economy should be organized around democratic cooperatives that "involve the masses in the management of public affairs."[45] Political as well as economic life should be as decentralized as possible. He doesn't even like the idea of political power being centered in the capital. Civil servants and bureaucrats should always be compelled to forge and renew their contact with the mass of the people, the peasants.

This is a very different image of social relations than existed in any African country after independence—including in Algeria. Fanon had long before taken issue with the single-party states adopted by reactionaries and clients of western imperialism, such as Felix Houphouet-Boigy of Ivory Coast. However, it was also endemic to regimes that Fanon worked closely with at times, such as Ghana, Guinea, and Mali. It is hard to read these passages and not see in them an implicit critique of some of his closest allies. The same is true of Algeria and the FLN, which exhibited all of the characteristics of the single-party-state-in-the-making that is criticized in *The Wretched of the Earth*.

This is not to suggest that as of 1961 Fanon has cut his ties to the more progressive African regimes. He has by no means given up on them. But neither is he writing any blank checks. His critique of the limits of the nationalist leadership of the African revolutions is in many respects analogous to Marx's critique of crude communism in his *Economic and Philosophical Manuscripts of 1844*.[46] Just as Marx posits a vision of "positive humanism, beginning from itself" through a critique of revolutionary allies, the crude communists, who think that the abolition of private property is sufficient to create the new society, so Fanon posits a vision of a "New Humanism" through a critique of revolutionary allies, the crude nationalists, who think that the abolition of colonial political domination is sufficient to create the new society. The dialectical structure of their respective arguments is very much the same.

The question that needs to be asked, however, is that if Fanon's critique of "The Trials and Tribulations of National Consciousness" reflects his concerns and growing disappointment with the Algerian Revolution why does he not make this explicit? Why does he refrain from any public criticism of the FLN—either in 1957, when Abane was murdered, or in 1961, by which time it was quite clear that the FLN was readying itself to impose a single-party state? It was no surprise to anyone when the FLN (not long after Fanon's death) formally imposed single-party state rule, in September 1963. So why did Fanon not explicitly voice his criticisms and concerns insofar as Algeria was concerned? The reason is that despite his criticism of centralism and hierarchical forms of organization he believed that it was imperative to maintain the unity of the movement in the face of imperialism. Speaking out would fracture that unity, and this option he could simply not entertain. Peter Geismar speaks to this as follows:

> He was aware of the grave differences of opinion within the [Algerian] revolution; he knew that rival power cliques had not hesitated to order liquidations within the nationalist ranks. But he didn't think it would serve a useful purpose to publicize the political fratricides that would eventually split open the whole movement. The friends of Fanon now living outside of Algeria state that at the very least Fanon was troubled when he spoke of the revolution after 1960.[47]

For us in the twenty-first century, it is no longer possible to maintain such a stance. We have witnessed too many tragic mishaps to permit it. In opposition to the insistence on keeping criticism of the defects of a movement private, virtually all the social movements that have arisen over the past three decades have emphasized the need for open and free democratic debate and airing of differences during the very course of the struggle. The same was true of the socialist and communist movements prior to Stalinism. In this sense, despite her persistent rejection of virtually all demands for national self-determination, Rosa Luxemburg stands higher than Fanon on this issue since she did not refrain from publicly criticizing the Bolsheviks for suppressing democracy and freedom of expression in 1918 even though they were severely threatened by imperialist aggression. She supported the Bolshevik seizure of power and never compromised with bourgeois society, but she did not refrain from issuing an open and public critique.[48] Her legacy had largely receded from view by the time of the national independence movements of the 1950s and 1960s, but that is not the case today. History performs its own auto-critique.

The Cold War and Non-Alignment

Fanon wanted nothing to with the Cold War and felt that it was a grave mistake for the newly independent countries to align themselves with either superpower. He writes, "An end must be put to this cold war that gets us nowhere, the nuclear arms race must be stopped and the underdeveloped regions must receive generous investments and technical aid."[49] Many others in the independence movements shared the principle of nonalignment and Fanon's comments about it are by no means original. More telling is his statement

> It was commonly thought that the time had come for the world, and particularly for the Third World, to choose between the capitalist system and the socialist system. The underdeveloped countries ... must, however, refuse to get involved in such rivalry. The Third World must not be content to define itself in relation to values that preceded it. On the contrary, the underdeveloped countries must endeavor to focus on their very own values as well as methods and style specific to them. The basic issue with which we are faced is not the unequivocal choice between socialism and capitalism such as they have been defined by men from different continents and different periods of time.[50]

Fanon wanted the newly independent countries to define *new* values for themselves, develop new social structures and ideas instead of following the ones hitherto defined by European society—whether capitalist or "socialist." This is a long way from the claim that he aspires for "the same life with the same aim [as] exists in the Soviet Union," as Adolfo Gilly asserted.[51] Fanon wants the African countries to maintain their distance from the superpowers because he aspires for a *new life* that surmounts the limitations of both "democratic" bourgeois societies and the dictatorships of the single-party states that *called* themselves "socialist."

Fanon is not always as clear-sighted in this issue in his other writings. For instance, in his notes for the effort to navigate the southern front, he wrote:

> With the triumph of socialism in Eastern Europe we witness a spectacular disappearance of the old rivalries, of the traditional claims. That nucleus of wars and political assassinations that Bulgaria, Hungary, Estonia, Albania represented, has made way for a coherent world whose objective is the building of a socialist society.[52]

Fanon was clearly wrong. The USSR's domination of Eastern Europe did not cause "old rivalries" to vanish—it merely suppressed them under a military occupation, while giving "great Russian chauvinism" a new lease on life. The thirst for national independence from Russian domination did not "disappear" in these Eastern European countries, and surely not in Poland (which is oddly not mentioned). Fanon expressed a very different point of view a few some months later, after returning from his medical treatment in the USSR. In addition to being horrified at Soviet medical and psychiatric practices, he complained to a friend, "The Russians and the Ukrainians see the Chechnyans and even the Georgians as barbarians."[53]

Nevertheless, Fanon never developed a clear and explicit critique of Soviet-type societies. As Cherki notes, he "really did not care to delve into a detailed analysis of the Soviet State. There were other things on his mind."[54] That is highly unfortunate, as it would have enabled him to more explicitly and adequately articulate the need for the independence movements to avoid becoming entrapped by concepts of "socialism" that stand in the way, and indeed contravene, his search for a "New Humanism."

Fanon and Islam

Fanon was more clear-sighted when it came to his understanding of the contributions of Islam as well as the danger of political Islamism. From his first entry into the Algerian political scene, Fanon took great pains to try to understand Islam and Algerian Moslem society— something he knew very little about upon his arrival. He traveled to rural areas to learn more about Islamic religious and cultural practices, both as part of his work as a psychiatrist and as an active revolutionary. He did not dismiss traditional practices and beliefs but tried to understand them and singled out those dimensions that had positive, even revolutionary features. And he certainly made no effort to impose his own atheistic orientation upon others that he worked with. He did not posit humanism in opposition to religion *tout court*, let alone Islam. That by no means signifies, however, that Fanon was not alert to the dangers of political Islamism within the national liberation movement. He had sided with Abane and the decisions of the Soummam Conference largely because of its effort to steer the movement away from those who wished to impose an Arab-Islamic instead of secular-socialist identity upon post-independence Algeria. His criticism of those who wished to move things in a different direction is made explicit in *The Wretched of the Earth*.

One of Fanon's main criticisms of the national-bourgeois stage of development is that the weakness and vacillation of the professional and business class signifies that it cannot succeed in creating any kind of organic *national* solidarity, let alone *African* unity. Hobbled by economic backwardness and political inexperience, the national bourgeoisie is incapable of uniting the people under a common emancipatory project. As a result, African unity founders—reducing the goal of Pan-Africanism to (at best) a utopian dream—while the nation-state begins to come apart at the seams. In sum, "because it cannot see further than the end of its own nose, the national bourgeoisie proves incapable of achieving simple national unity and incapable of building the nation on a solid, constructive foundation."[55] This process of national (and continental) disintegration, he held, opens the door to some of the most regressive tendencies imaginable—including religious fundamentalism.

> This ruthless struggle waged by the ethnic groups and tribes, and this virulent obsession with filling the vacancies left by the foreigners also engender religious rivalries. In the interior and the bush, the minor confraternities, the local religions, and *marabout* cults spring back to life and resort once more to the vicious circle of mutual denunciation. In the urban centers the authorities are confronted with a clash between the two major revealed religions: Islam and Catholicism.[56]

It bears noting that though colonialism bears a good measure of blame for this—and neocolonialism surely tries to make use of these divisions for its own purposes—the rise of religious hatred and fanaticism is most of all an *internal* phenomenon resulting from the limitations *within* the anti-colonial struggle. Foremost among these is the failure to complete the revolutionary process, to push it beyond the fickle bourgeois stage. He writes

> Within the same nation, religion divides the people and sets the spiritual communities, fostered and encouraged by colonialism and its apparatus, at odds with each other. Totally unexpected events break out here and there. In predominantly Catholic or Protestant countries the Muslim minority redoubles its religious fervor. Muslim festivals are revived and Islam defends itself every inch of the way . . . [57]

There is absolutely no evidence that Fanon ever entertained the idea of making alliances with political Islamism or that he held that there were tendencies within Islamic fundamentalism that should be sought out as potential allies against imperialism. This does not mean that he dismisses out of hand "a cultural phenomenon commonly known as the awakening of Islam."[58] Reminding others of the contributions of your religious heritage is not inherently regressive. What *is* regressive is when this enters the terrain of political struggle through an unabashed embrace of the "traditional." The revival of atavistic tribal and religious identity is a function of the breakdown of the revolution, of its impending failure, not of its potential resurrection.

Fanon therefore went out of his way to make it clear that citizenship in an independent Algeria must not be based on religion, ethnicity or race. "The people" refers to those who become part of the project of national independence and reconstruction—the Jews as much as the Muslims, the Europeans as much as the Arabs, the Kayble people as much as those of any other national minority. Politics based on religious identity never held any attraction for Fanon, and least of all when it came to the Algerian situation.

Near the end of his life Fanon spelled out some of his views on Islam with the Iranian thinker Ali Shariati, who later published a volume of Fanon's writings in Farsi. Fanon wrote, "I respect your view that in the Third World (and if you don't mind, I would prefer to say in the Near and Middle East), Islam, more than any other social and ideological force, has had an anti-colonialist capacity and an anti-Western nature." However, he added, "I, for one, fear that the fact of revitalizing the spirit of sectarianism and religion may result in a setback for a nation that is engaged in the process of becoming, of distancing itself from its future and immobilizing it in its past."[59]

These are prophetic words—not alone in anticipating later developments in the Arab world but also of the Iranian revolution of 1979. Those who apologize or make excuses for Islamic fundamentalism and its regressive agenda will find no comfort in the thought of Fanon—his writings on violence notwithstanding. And those who seek alliances or compromises with political Islamism—on the grounds that it is an "understandable" reaction to "Western imperialism"—will find no support within his body of thought either. Few modern thinkers were more adamantly opposed to colonialism and imperialism than Fanon, but few were also more critical of the internal contradictions and limitations within putatively "anti-imperialist" movements. The text of Fanon's last book is living proof of that.

What is clear from Fanon's body of work as a whole is that he never endorsed any movement or strategy based on *ressentiment* and the vile thirst to negate for the sake of negation. His theoretical and political compass was always directed at the creation of a new humanity based on the brotherhood of peoples. He never gave up believing in human solidarity—even as he wondered whether it was possible for a truly human world to arise from the ashes of racism and colonialism. He is aware that the freedom struggle is a delicate matter, easily distorted and destroyed when its aims are confused or left aside. And this is also why Fanon understands that counterrevolution can easily take on seemingly "revolutionary" features—a problem the he directly warns against in *The Wretched of the Earth*:

There is a brutality and contempt for subtleties and individual cases that is typically revolutionary, but there is another type of brutality with surprising resemblances to the first one that is typically counterrevolutionary, adventurist, and anarchist. If this pure, total brutality is not immediately contained it will, without fail, bring down the movement within a few weeks.[60]

Even with all of his criticisms of the limitations within the national movements, Fanon would no doubt have been shocked at the degree of regression that engulfed much of Africa in the years after he wrote his last book. National liberation descended into ideological and political discord between tribes and religions, only in due time to descend even further, in such places as Liberia, Sierra Leone, and the Congo, into incessant battles over resources by armed groups that lacked even the fig leaf of ideology or political purpose. This unraveling is, however, anticipated by the logic of the analysis contained in *The Wretched of the Earth*. But it is not only his warning of tragic mishaps to come that makes him an important thinker but also his insistence that "The urgent thing is to rediscover what is important beneath what is contingent."[61] By making us aware of the revolutionary possibilities that exists in *his* moment, for all its risks and uncertainties, his approach can make us aware of the revolutionary possibilities existing in *ours*.

Fanon's Vision of Human Emancipation

Fanon projects a magnificent vision of human liberation in the final chapters of *The Wretched of the Earth*. Some of his most poignant discussion appears in "The Trials and Tribulations of National Consciousness." He writes

> We have seen in the preceding pages how nationalism, that magnificent hymn which roused the masses against the oppressor, disintegrates in the aftermath of independence. Nationalism is not a political doctrine, it is not a program. If we really want to safeguard our countries from regression, paralysis, or collapse, we

must rapidly switch from a national consciousness to a social and political consciousness.[62]

We have already seen that with *The Wretched of the Earth*, Fanon goes beyond envisioning a form of black essentialism (such as negritude) as the mediating term in the movement from the individual to the universal in emphasizing the national liberation struggle of the masses. He now peers beyond that mediation, into the universal itself. A higher stage of self-consciousness is needed than even national consciousness—that of a thoroughgoing social and political transformation that illuminates the content of a new society. Fanon was always interested in looking beyond the immediacy of the struggle and envisioning its ultimate goals, even before its most immediate goals were met. He struggled with others in the Algerian movement over this issue from the moment he joined it. This comes to a culmination in *The Wretched of the Earth*, where he projects the challenge of envisioning *what happens after the revolution before it occurs.*

This remains the fundamental, unanswered question facing all freedom movements today—and not alone those fighting for national self-determination or against racism. There is no more important question to answer for *our* time—especially for those trying to seek a path out of the dead-end of globalized capitalism (as well as its failed "alternatives" that anointed itself as statist "socialism").[63] Characteristically, Fanon does not allow us to race ahead to an answer as to "what happens after" that would skip over or deny the national liberation struggle. "The Africans and the underdeveloped peoples, contrary to what is commonly believed, are quick to build a social and political consciousness. The danger is that very often they reach the stage of social consciousness before reaching the national phase."[64]

As always, Fanon never lets us forget the particular, even when trying to orientate our gaze toward the universal. Skipping over the national phase would prove especially egregious in Africa, he warns, as it leaves the door open to tribalism and ethnic rivalry. National unity and national development are imperative—even more imperative than abstract calls for Pan-Africanism. At the same time, "we must not expect the nation to produce new men."[65] The creation and formation of the nation is not an end in itself, but a conduit to something else. In sum, "If nationalism is not explained, enriched, and deepened, if it does not very quickly turn into a social and political consciousness, into humanism, then it leads to a dead end. A bourgeois leadership of the underdeveloped countries confines the national consciousness to a sterile formalism."[66]

Fanon never so much as mentions Hegel in *The Wretched of the Earth*, but the attentive reader will notice that the Hegelian dialectic of individual-particular-universal forms the structure of the work's central argument. What is of foremost importance in the dialectical movement from the lived experience of the specific individual to the universal goal of mutual recognition is the *mediating* term. This mediating term must be integral to the living individual at the same time as capable of directing it beyond itself. In this sense, mediation for Hegel represents a kind of conflict of forces—it interposes itself between the individual experiences of the subject and the ultimate goal that can *realize* its subjectivity. As Hegel puts it, "what is meant by [mediation] is in general the demand for the *realization of the Notion*, which realization does not lie in the *beginning* itself, but is rather the goal and the task of the entire further development of cognition."[67] For Fanon, the mediating term that can actualize the subjectivity of the individual subject is the struggle for national liberation. This mediating term, however, is not an end-in-itself, since it points the way to a *further development* of the movement of liberation. It is not the number of explicit references to Hegel that makes a work dialectical, but rather its philosophical content and structure. In some respects, it can be argued that *The Wretched of the Earth* is even *more* Hegelian than *Black Skin, White Masks* insofar as the former's political-revolutionary content posits a more concrete form of subjective mediation than the latter, at the same time as it probes deeper into the universal goal that is implied by the battle for recognition.

Fanon peers even further into what that universal goal consists of in the chapter "Colonial War and Mental Disorders," writing:

Fighting for the freedom of one's people is not the only necessity. As long as the fight goes on you must enlighten not only the people but also, and above all, yourself on the full measure of man. You must retrace the paths of history, the history of man damned by other men, and initiate, bring about, the encounter between your own people and others.[68]

Fanon's central philosophical message is that instead of trying to copy or catch up with Europe, it is time to leave it behind—not because all of the values and ideas that arose from it were necessarily wrong, but because they remained unrealized by a Europe which speaks of "man" while slaughtering man *en masse*. Europe has failed humanity; but humanity is not a failure.[69] Its renewal *is* possible.

Comrades, let us flee this stagnation where dialectics has gradually turned into a logic of the status quo. Let us reexamine the question of man . . . No, we do not want to catch up with anyone. What we want is to walk in the company of man, every man, night and day, for all times. It is not a question of stringing the caravan out where groups are spaced so far apart that they cannot see the one in front, and men who no longer recognize each other, meet less and less and talk to each other less and less.[70]

Today, in the aftermath of the "triumph" of capitalist globalization and the failure of innumerable revolutions around the world—not to mention the everyday atomization of life that has destroyed so much of *our* public space—we are spaced far apart indeed. We seem to have lost our way and know not where to turn. If there is anything to be gained from a study of Fanon, it is to become oriented once again to that goal that makes life meaningful—the struggle to create new human relations. There could be no greater tribute to Fanon's legacy than for us to recapture *our* humanism from the realm of absolute alienation that pervades our time. It is a challenge that can be taken up regardless of one's particular situation or vantage point. The universe may not be contained in a grain of sand, but the universal can be pursued from even the smallest grain of dissatisfaction with existing conditions.

History is replete with examples of freedom struggles that lost their way because they took their eyes off the universal. What makes

Fanon's work so important today, half a century after his death, is that it is replete with warnings and direction about how *not* to lose sight of it. Although Fanon developed his ideas from the zero point of his orientation, there is nothing that stops us from reaching for a new humanism from the zero point of *our* orientation. A movement is "Fanonian" not because it consists of peasants, lumpenproletarians, or shackdwellers, any more than it is "Fanonian" because it consists of the working class, students, women, gays and lesbians, or blacks and other national minorities. A movement is "Fanonian" insofar, and only insofar, as it "reexamines the question of humanity," rejuvenates it, and *actualizes* it.

Fanon did not live to do so. After arriving in the U.S. for medical treatment, he died on December 6, 1961—three days after *The Wretched of the Earth* was published. The journey is now ours to take.

Notes

Introduction

1. For one many of the many commentators who cited Fanon's statement, see Jerome Roos in RoarMag.org of December 7, 2014 [http://roarmag.org/2014/12/eric-garner-protests-we-cant-breathe].

2. Frantz Fanon, *The Wretched of the Earth*, translated by Richard Philcox (New York: Grove Press, 2008), p. 201.

3. Frantz Fanon, *Black Skin, White Masks*, translated by Richard Philcox (New York: Grove Press, 2004), p. 5.

4. Fanon, *Black Skin, White Masks*, p. 202.

5. Fanon, *The Wretched of the Earth*, p. 2.

6. Fanon, *Black Skin, White Masks*, p. 69.

7. Ibid., p. xii.

8. Ibid., p. 24.

9. Ibid., p. 206.

10. Lewis Gordon, *Fanon and the Crisis of European Man: An Essay on Philosophy and the Human Sciences* (London and New York: Routledge, 1995), p. 58.

11. Fanon, *Black Skin, White Masks*, p. xi.

12. Ibid., p. 193.

13. Henry Lewis Gates, "Critical Fanonism," in Nigel C. Gibson (ed.), *Rethinking Fanon: The Continuing Dialogue* (Amherst, NY: Humanities Books, 1999).

14. Adolfo Gilly, "Introduction" to Frantz Fanon, *A Dying Colonialism* (New York: Grove Press, 1967), p. 13.

15. Fanon, *The Wretched of the Earth*, p. 235.

16. Quoted in David Macey, *Frantz Fanon: A Biography* (London and New York: Verso, 2012), p. 21.

17. Hannah Arendt, *On Violence* (New York: Harcourt, Brace and World, 1969), p. 71.

18. Maurice Merleau-Ponty, *Phenomenology of Perception* (London and New York: Routledge, 2004), p. 44.

19. See *Black Skin, White Masks*, p, 119: "I feel my soul as vast as the world, truly a soul as deep as the deepest of rivers; my chest has the power to

expand to infinity. I was made to give and they prescribe for me the humility of the cripple."

20. Merleau-Ponty, *Phenomenology of Perception*, pp. xvii, xviii.

21. For Merleau-Ponty, a "bodily-schema" is the summation of our corporeal experience, "a way of stating that my body is in-the-world." See *Phenomenology of Perception*, p. 115.

22. G.W.F. Hegel, *Phenomenology of Spirit*, translated by A.V. Miller (Oxford: Oxford University Press, 1977), p. 480.

23. Ibid., p. 110.

24. For Marx's writings on developing countries at the end of his life, in which he singled out the revolutionary role of the peasantry and denied that Volume One of *Capital* constituted a "universal theory" for the entire world's development, see Peter Hudis, "Marx Among the Muslims," *Capitalism, Nature, Socialism*, Vol. 15, No. 4, December 2004, pp. 51–68; Peter Hudis, "Accumulation, Imperialism, and Pre-Capitalist Formations," *Socialist Studies/Études socialistes*, Vol. 6, No. 2, Fall 2010, pp. 75–91; and Kevin B. Anderson, *Marx at the Margins: On Nationalism, Ethnicity, and Non-Western Societies* (Chicago: University of Chicago Press, 2010).

25. Fanon, *The Wretched of the Earth*, p. xi.

26. Fanon, *Black Skin, White Masks*, p. xiv.

27. Ibid., p. xii.

Chapter 1

1. Rosa Luxemburg, "Martinique," in Peter Hudis and Kevin B. Anderson (eds.), *The Rosa Luxemburg Reader* (New York: Monthly Review Books, 2004), pp. 123–4.

2. Frantz Fanon, "The Problem of the Colonized," in *Toward the African Revolution*, translated by Haakon Chevalier (New York: Grove Press, 1967), p. 18.

3. See Stuart Hall, "Cultural Identity and Diaspora," in Bill Ashcroft, Gareth Griffiths, and Helen Tiffin (eds.), *The Post-Colonial Studies Reader* (London and New York: Routledge, 2006), p. 436.

4. Quoted by Alice Cherki, *Frantz Fanon: A Portrait*, translated by Nadia Benabid (Ithaca and London: Cornell University Press, 2006), p. 1.

5. Ibid., p. 8.

6. Fanon, "The Problem of the Colonized," in *Toward the African Revolution*, p. 23.

7. Fanon, *The Wretched of the Earth*, p. 2.

8. Fanon, "The Problem of the Colonized," in *Toward the African Revolution*, p. 23.

9. For more on this, see Irene L. Gendzier, *Frantz Fanon: A Critical Study* (New York: Pantheon Books, 1973), pp. 39–43 and Irving Leonard Markovitz, *Léopold Sédar Senghor and the Politics of Negritude* (New York: Atheneum, 1969), pp. 40–58.

10. Fanon, "The Problem of the Colonized," in *Toward the African Revolution*, p. 24.

11. These words were later recounted by Manville; see Cherki, *Frantz Fanon: A Portrait*, p. 10.

12. Quoted in Fanon, *Black Skin, White Masks*, pp. 69–70. See Karl Jaspers, *The Question of German Guilt*, translated by E.B. Aston (New York: Greenwood, Press, 1978), p. 32.

13. A curious irony, given that his mother's maternal grandfather was Alsatian, from which Fanon received his Germanic first name.

14. Quoted in Macey, *Frantz Fanon: A Biography*, p. 101.

15. For more on this, see Peter Geismar, *Fanon* (New York: The Dial Press, 1971), pp. 41–2.

16. See Raya Dunayevskaya, "Dialectics: The Algebra of Revolution," in *The Raya Dunayevskaya Collection: Marxist-Humanism—A Half Century of its World Development* (Detroit: Wayne State University Archives of Labor History and Urban Affairs), microfilm no. 5791.

17. Geismar, *Fanon*, p. 46.

18. See Fanon, *Black Skin, White Masks*, p. 42: "This book represents seven years of experiments and observations."

19. See Cherki, *Frantz Fanon: A Portrait*, p. 136.

20. Macey, *Frantz Fanon: A Biography*, p. 147.

21. Quoted in Geismar, p. 54. *Fanon*.

22. Fanon, "The North African Syndrome," in *Toward the African Revolution*, p. 3.

23. Ibid., p. 13.

24. Fanon, *Black Skin, White Masks*, p. 206.

25. See Marx, *Economic and Philosophical Manuscripts of 1844*, in *Marx and Engels Collected Works*, Vol. 3 (New York: International Publishers, 1975), pp. 277: "Estranged labor turns thus *Man's species-being*, both nature and his spiritual species-property, into a being *alien* to him, into a *means* for his *individual existence*. It estranges man from his own body, as well as external nature and his spiritual aspect, his *human* aspect."

26. G.W.F. Hegel, *Science of Logic* Vol. 2, translated by W.H. Johnston and L.G. Struthers (New York: The Macmillan Company, 1929), p. 411.

27. Fanon, "The 'North African Syndrome," in *Toward the African Revolution*, p. 15. The emphasis is Fanon's.

Chapter 2

1. See Aime Césaire, *Discourse on Colonialism*, translated by Joan Pinkham (New York: Monthly Review Books, 2000), p. 36.

2. Fanon, *Black Skin, White Masks*, p. xii.

3. Ibid., p. 97.

4. Ibid., p. 89.

5. Ibid., p. xii.

6. Dante, *The Inferno*, translated by Laurence Binyon, in *The Portable Dante* (New York: Viking Press, 1948), p. 3.

7. Fanon, *Black Skin, White Masks*, p. 2.

8. Ibid., p. xi.

9. Ibid., pp. 91, 165.

10. Ibid., p. 95.

11. Ibid., p. 90.

12. Ato Sekyi-Otu, *Fanon's Dialectic of Experience* (Cambridge: Harvard University Press, 1996), p. 63.

13. Jean-Paul Sartre, *Being and Nothingness*, translated by Hazel E. Barnes (New York: Washington Square Press, 1969), p. 553.

14. Fanon, *Black Skin, White Masks*, p. 90.

15. Karel Kosik, *Dialectics of the Concrete: A Study on the Problem of Man and World* (Dordrecht-Holland: D. Reidel, 1976), p. 7.

16. Fanon, *Black Skin, White Masks*, p. 205.

17. Ibid., p. xiv.

18. Ibid., pp. 120–1.

19. Ibid., p. 122.

20. Ibid., p. xv.

21. Ibid., p. 165.

22. Ibid., p. 130.

23. For more on this, see Cherki, *Frantz Fanon: A Portrait*, who argues that "to cast Fanon as a black Lacan . . . [is] the product of pure delusion" (p. 199).

24. Fanon, *Black Skin, White Masks*, p. xv.

25. Ibid.

26. For more on Fanon's view of Reich, which he related on various occasions in oral discussions with friends and colleagues, see Cherki, *Frantz Fanon: A Portrait*, pp. 35–6.

27. Fanon, *Black Skin, White Masks*, p. xv.

28. Ibid., p. 25

29. For more on Capécia and other long-neglected women writers associated with the negritude movement, see T. Denean Sharpley-Whiting, *Frantz Fanon: Conflicts and Feminisms* (Lanham: Rowman & Littlefield, 1998), p. 36.

30. Fanon, *Black Skin, White Masks*, p. 26.

31. Ibid., p. 27.

32. Ibid., p. 44.

33. Ibid., p. 35.

34. Ibid., p. 24.

35. Ibid., p. 42.

36. Ibid., p. 56.

37. Ibid., p. 61.

38. Ibid., p. 69.

39. Cherki, *Frantz Fanon: A Portrait*, p. 88.

40. Fanon, *Black Skin, White Masks*, p. 66.

41. See Derrick Bell, *Faces at the Bottom of the Well: The Permanence of Racism* (New York: Basic Books, 1992).

42. Fanon, *Black Skin, White Masks*, p. 80.

43. Ibid., p. 63.

44. Hegel, *Phenomenology of Spirit*, p. 110.

45. Peter Kalkavage, *The Logic of Desire: An Introduction to Hegel's Phenomenology of Spirit* (Philadelphia: Paul Dry Books, 2007), p. 98.

46. Hegel, *Phenomenology of Spirit*, p. 106.

47. See Alex Honneth, *The Struggle for Recognition: The Moral Grammar of Social Conflicts* (Cambridge: Polity Press, 1995) and *The I in We: Studies in the Theory of Recognition* (Cambridge: Polity Press, 2012).

48. Fanon, *Black Skin, White Masks*, p. 14.

49. Henri Lefebvre, "The Inventory," in Stuart Elden, Elizabeth Lebas, and Eleonore Kofman (eds.), *Henri Lefebvre: Key Writings* (New York and London: Continuum, 2003), pp. 175–6.

50. Hegel, *Phenomenology of Spirit*, p. 110.

51. Kalkavage, *The Logic of Desire*, p. 121.

52. Fanon, *Black Skin, White Masks*, p. 191.

53. Ibid., p. 192.

54. For a different perspective that argues that Hegel did base his discussion of the master/slave dialectic on an understanding of race and the Haitian revolution, see Susan Buck-Morss, *Hegel, Haiti, and Universal History* (Pittsburgh: University of Pittsburg Press, 2009).

55. This is confirmed by the fact that what follows the master/slave dialectic in Hegel is a discussion of stoicism and skepticism—the major philosophies of the ancient Greek and Roman world.

56. Fanon, *Black Skin, White Masks*, p. 195.

57. Ibid.

58. Ibid., p. 185.

59. For more on this, see Raya Dunayevskaya, "Hegel, Marx, Lenin, Fanon and the Dialectics of Liberation Today," in Peter Hudis and Kevin B. Anderson (eds.), *The Power of Negativity: Selected Writings on the Dialectic in Hegel and Marx* (Lanham, MD: Lexington Books, 2006), p. 193.

60. Fanon, *Black Skin, White Masks*, p. 196.

61. Hegel, *Phenomenology of Spirit*, p. 119.

62. Fanon, *Black Skin, White Masks*, p. 33.

63. Ibid., p. 95.

64. Ibid., p. 101.

65. Ibid., p. 112.

66. Ibid.

67. Ibid., p. 114.

68. Ibid., p. 113.

69. Ibid., p. 107.

70. Ibid., pp. 113-14.

71. See Hegel, *Phenomenology of Spirit*, p. 10: "In my view, which can be justified only by the exposition of the system itself, everything turns on grasping and expressing the True, not only as *Substance*, but equally as *Subject*." Not only—but not *instead* as!

72. Fanon, *Black Skin, White Masks*, p. 17.

73. Ibid., p. 101.

74. Ibid., p. 102.

75. Ibid., p. 98.

76. For more on this, see Raya Dunayevskaya, *Philosophy and Revolution: from Hegel to Sartre and from Marx to Mao* (Lanham, MD: Lexington Books, 2003), pp. 3–46.

77. Sekyi-Otu, *Fanon's Dialectic of Experience*, p. 201.

78. Fanon, *The Wretched of the Earth*, p. 179.

Chapter 3

1. Fanon, *Black Skin, White Masks*, p. 101.
2. Cherki, *Frantz Fanon: A Portrait*, p. 43.
3. Ibid., p. 61.
4. The claim of Fanon unchaining his patients is found in Gendzier, *Frantz Fanon: A Critical Study*, p. 76. See Macey, *Frantz Fanon: A Biography*, p. 225, for a refutation of the claim.
5. Quoted in Cherki, *Frantz Fanon: A Portrait*, p. 69.
6. Quoted in Gendzier, *Frantz Fanon: A Critical Study*, p. 81.
7. Ibid., p. 88.
8. Ibid., p. 82.
9. Macey, *Fanon: A Biography*, p. 236.
10. An excellent study of these writings, in the context of a fine evaluation of Fanon's thought as a whole, is found in Hussein Abdilahi Bulhan, *Frantz Fanon and the Psychology of Oppression* (New York: Plenum Press, 1985).
11. Bulhan, *Frantz Fanon and the Psychology of Oppression*, p. 229.
12. Hegel, *Phenomenology of Spirit*, pp. 407–8.
13. Fanon, "Racism and Culture," in *Toward the African Revolution*, p. 38.
14. Ibid., p. 40.
15. Ibid., pp. 41, 43.
16. Karl Marx, *Capital* Vol. 3, translated by David Fernbach (New York: Penguin, 1981), p. 959.
17. Cherki, *Frantz Fanon: A Portrait*, pp. 34, 35.
18. Macey, *Frantz Fanon: A Biography*, p. 320.
19. Ibid., p. 323.

Chapter 4

1. For the events leading up to the formation of the FLN, see Henry F. Jackson, *The FLN in Algeria: Party Development in a Revolutionary Society* (Westport. CN: Greenwood Press, 1977), pp. 22–43.
2. For the early history of the Algerian national liberation movement, see Jackson, *The FLN in Algeria*, pp. 3–21.
3. Rosa Luxemburg, *The Accumulation of Capital*, in Peter Hudis and Paul Le Blanc (eds.) *The Complete Works of Rosa Luxemburg* Vol. II: Economic Writings 2 (London and New York: Verso Books, 2015), pp. 271, 274.

4. See Salim Nadi, "Why Do We Need an Indigenous Party in France?" Paper Presented to Historical Materialism Conference, London England, November 28, 2014, p. 4.

5. For more on this, see Cherki, *Frantz Fanon: A Portrait*, pp. 78–80. Cherki directly worked with Fanon during this period and she is the best source for how he became active with the FLN.

6. Fanon, "West Indians and Africans," in *Toward the African Revolution*, p. 18.

7. Ibid., p. 24.

8. Ibid., pp. 26–7.

9. See Fanon, *Black Skin, White Masks* in discussing Mayotte Capécia: "Apparently for her, Black and White represent the two poles of this world, poles in perpetual conflict: a genuinely Manichaean notion of the world" (p. 27).

10. Quoted in Macey, *Frantz Fanon: A Biography*, p. 270.

11. Quoted in Cherki, *Frantz Fanon: A Portrait*, pp. 101–2.

12. "Racism and Culture," in *Toward the African Revolution*, p. 35.

13. Ibid., p. 40.

14. Ibid., p. 43.

15. Ibid.

16. Ibid.

17. Ibid., p. 44.

18. See Cherki, *Frantz Fanon: A Portrait*, p. 93.

19. Several volumes of these proceedings are now available in English, thanks to the tireless work of John Riddell. See his *Workers of the World and Oppressed Peoples, Unite!: Proceedings and Documents of the Second Congress, 1920* (New York: Pathfinder, 1991); *Toward the United Front: Proceedings of the Fourth Congress of the Communist International* (Leiden and Boston: Brill, 2011) and *To the Masses: Proceedings of the Third Congress of the Communist International* (Leiden and Boston: Brill, 2014).

20. In *The Wretched of the Earth*, Fanon writes, "above all Budapest and Suez constituted the deciding moments of this confrontation" (p. 38)—that is, the confrontation between the Western powers and USSR. But he expresses no position on the revolution itself.

21. For more on this, see Peter Hudis (ed.) *The Marxist-Humanist Theory of State-Capitalism: Selected Writings by Raya Dunayevskaya* (Chicago: News and Letters, 1992), pp. 103–8 and 115–22.

22. "Letter to the Resident Minister," in *Toward the African Revolution*, p. 52.

23. See Gendzier, *Frantz Fanon: A Critical Study*, p. 142.

24. See Macey, *Frantz Fanon: A Biography*, p. 331.

25. "Algeria Face to Face with the French Torturers," in *Toward the African Revolution*, p. 65.

26. "Concerning a Plea," in *Toward the African Revolution*, p. 74.

27. Fanon, "French Intellectuals and Democrats and the Algerian Revolution," in *Toward the African Revolution*, p. 76.

28. See Anderson, *Marx at the Margins*, pp. 9–41 and 196–236.

29. For more on this, see Macey, *Frantz Fanon: A Biography*, pp. 338–9.

30. See Eugene V. Debs, "Danger Ahead," *International Socialist Review*, Vol. 4, No. 5, November 1903: "We have simply to open the eyes of as many Negroes as we can and bring them into the Socialist movement to do battle for emancipation from wage slavery, and when the working class have triumphed in the class struggle and stand forth economic as well as political free men, the race problem will forever disappear." Debs was of course a principled opponent of racism, but he did not grasp the *independent* role of the struggle of the black masses against it.

31. For a fine criticism of the failures of the U.S. radical left in this regard, see Michael C. Dawson, *Blacks In and Out of the Left* (Cambridge: Harvard University Press, 2013).

32. This included the *Socialisme ou Barbarie* group, which Fanon knew of but expressed little interest in. For more on this, see Cherki, *Frantz Fanon: A Portrait*, p. 95.

33. "French Intellectuals and Democrats and the Algerian Revolution," in *Toward the African Revolution*, p. 87.

34. Ibid., p. 88.

35. Fanon, "The Algerian War and Man's Liberation," in *Toward the African Revolution*, p. 144.

36. Ibid.

37. Fanon, *The Wretched of the Earth*, p. 62.

38. See Cornelius Castoriadis, "General Introduction" in *Political and Social Writings, Vol. I, 1946–1955: From the Critique of Bureaucracy to the Positive Content of Socialism* (Minneapolis: University of Minnesota Press, 1988), p. 25. Castoriadis also accuses Fanon of "Third World messianism" in "The Diversionists," *Telos*, No. 33, 1977, p. 105. Castoriadis does not appear to have shown any real interest in the Algerian struggle.

39. Fanon, "French Intellectuals and Democrats and the Algerian Revolution," in *Toward the African Revolution*, pp. 81-2.

40. Ibid., p. 81.

41. Fanon, *A Dying Colonialism*, pp. 152–3.

42. Fanon, *The Wretched of the Earth*, p. 95.

43. Sekyi-Otu, *Fanon's Dialectic of Experience*, p. 116.

44. Fanon, "Decolonization and Independence," in *Toward the African Revolution*, p. 103.

45. See Fanon's "Appeal to Africans" in *Toward the African Revolution*, pp. 132–4.

46. Quoted in Cherki, *Frantz Fanon: A Portrait*, pp. 105, 112.

47. Ibid., p. 124.

48. For more on this, see Macey, *Frantz Fanon: A Biography*, p. 353.

Chapter 5

1. Fanon, "Accra: Africa Affirms Its Unity and Defines its Strategy," in *Toward the African Revolution*, p. 155.

2. Fanon, *The Wretched of the Earth*, p. 178.

3. Ibid., p. 169.

4. Ibid., p. 179.

5. Hegel, *Phenomenology of Spirit*, p. 10.

6. See Fanon, *Black Skin, White Masks*, pp. 113–14.

7. Fanon, *The Wretched of the Earth*, p. 180.

8. Ibid., pp. 163, 167.

9. Ibid., p. 179.

10. Gendzier, *Frantz Fanon: A Critical Study*, p. 226.

11. Ibid., p. 167.

12. Ibid., p. 229.

13. Marx, "Private Property and Communism," in *Economic and Philosophic Manuscripts of 1844*, p. 294.

14. Antonio Gramsci, *Selections from the Prison Notebooks*, translated by Quintin Hoare (New York: International Publishers, 1971), p. 405.

15. Fanon, *A Dying Colonialism*, p. 119.

16. Ibid., p. 24.

17. Ibid., p. 25.

18. Ibid., p. 32.

19. Ibid., pp. 57–8.

20. Hegel, *Phenomenology of Spirit*, p. 19.

21. Fanon, *A Dying Colonialism*, pp. 61, 62, 63.

22. Ibid., p. 63.

23. Fanon, *Black Skin, White Masks*, p. 205.

24. Fanon, *A Dying Colonialism*, p. 63.

25. Fanon, *Black Skin, White Masks*, p. 191.

26. Fanon, *A Dying Colonialism*, p. 44.

27. Ibid., p. 63.

28. Ibid., p. 107.

29. Ibid., p. 113.

30. Ibid., p. 92.

31. Ibid., p. 90.

32. Ibid., p. 95.

33. I am borrowing this phrase from Lenin's "Abstract of Hegel's *Science of Logic*," written in 1914–15. See Lenin's *Collected Works* Vol. 38 (London: Lawrence and Wishart, 1961), p. 212.

34. Dunayevskaya, *Philosophy and Revolution*, p. 13.

35. See Rosa Luxemburg, "The Mass Strike, the Political Party, and the Trade Unions," in *The Rosa Luxemburg Reader*, p. 185.

36. See Macey, *Frantz Fanon: A Biography*, pp. 392–3.

37. For more on this, see Cherki, *Frantz Fanon: A Portrait*, p. 127.

38. Much of the secondary literature on Fanon gives a wrong date for his appointment as ambassador. For one of many examples, see Carole Boyce Davies (ed.), *Encyclopedia of the African Diaspora* (Santa Barbara, CA: ABC-CLIO, 2008), p. 429, which says he became ambassador in 1957.

39. For a recent discussion of this turbulent period, see David Van Reybrouck, *Congo: The Epic History of a People* (New York: HarperCollins, 2014).

40. Fanon, "Lumumba's Death: Could We Do Otherwise?" in *Toward the African Revolution*, p. 196.

41. Ibid., p. 192.

42. Quoted by Cherki, *Frantz Fanon: A Portrait*, p. 149.

43. Fanon, "This Africa to Come," in *Toward the African Revolution*, pp. 180–1.

Chapter 6

1. For more on this, see Jackson, *The FLN in Algeria*, pp. 40–3.

2. Cherki, *Fanon: A Portrait*, p. 158.

3. See Gendzier, *Fanon: A Critical Study*, pp. 239–43.

4. Fanon, *The Wretched of the Earth*, p. 35.

5. Ibid., p. 120.

6. Ibid., p. 107.

7. Ibid., p. 103.

8. Ibid., p. 1.

9. Ibid., p. 2.

10. See Jackson, *The FLN in Algeria*, p. 209.

11. Fanon, *The Wretched of the Earth*, p. 97.

12. Sekyi-Otu, *Fanon's Dialectic of Experience*, p. 150.

13. Fanon, *The Wretched of the Earth*, p. 100.

14. Fanon, "This Africa to Come," in *Toward the African Revolution*, p. 187.

15. Fanon, *The Wretched of the Earth*, p. 109.

16. Ibid., p. 118.

17. Ibid., p. 119.

18. For a collection that shows the widespread discussion of this issue in the period from 1902 to 1906, see Richard B. Day and Daniel Gaido (eds.), *Witness to Permanent Revolution: The Documentary Record* (Chicago: Haymarket, 2009).

19. See Stephen White, "Communism and the East: The Baku Congress, 1920," *Slavic Review*, Vol. 33, No. 2, Summer 1974, pp. 492–514.

20. Fanon, *The Wretched of the Earth*, p. 119.

21. Ibid., p. 221.

22. Ibid., p. 17.

23. David Macey, *Frantz Fanon: A Biography*, p. 202.

24. Geismar, *Fanon*, p. 179.

25. See Cherki, *Frantz Fanon: A Portrait*. These are Cherki's words; Fanon cites Engels's work in *The Wretched of the Earth* (p. 25) but says little about it.

26. Fanon, *The Wretched of the Earth*, p. 51.

27. See Marnia Lazreg, *Torture and the Twilight of Empire: From Algiers to Bahgdad* (Princeton: Princeton University Press, 2008), p. 219.

28. Fanon, *The Wretched of the Earth*, p. 23.

29. Ibid., p. 69.

30. Ibid., p. 76.

31. Ibid., p. 73.

32. Ibid., p. 87.

33. For more on this, see Teodor Shanin (ed.) *Late Marx and the Russian Road: Marx and "The Peripheries of Capitalism"* (New York: Monthly Review Books, 1983).

34. Karl Marx and Frederick Engels, *The Communist Manifesto*, in *Marx and Engels Collected Works*, Vol. 6 (New York: International Publishers, 1976), p. 495.

35. For an especially crude example of such a critique of Fanon, see Jack Woodis, *New Theories of Revolution: A Commentary on the Views of Frantz Fanon, Régis Debray, and Herbert Marcuse* (New York: International Publishers, 1972).

36. Gramsci, *Selections from the Prison Notebooks*, p. 437.

37. Fanon, *The Wretched of the Earth*, p. 64.
38. For more on this, see Nigel Gibson, *Fanonian Practices in South Africa: from Steve Biko to Abahlali baseMjondolo* (New York: Palgrave Macmillan, 2011).
39. Fanon, *The Wretched of the Earth*, p. 111.
40. Ibid., p. 115.
41. Ibid., p. 127.
42. Ibid., p. 124
43. Ibid., p. 130.
44. Ibid., p. 138.
45. Ibid., p. 124.
46. See "Private Property and Communism," in *Marx and Engels Collected Works* Vol, 3, pp. 294–6.
47. Geismar, *Fanon*, p. 174.
48. See Rosa Luxemburg, *The Russian Revolution*, in *The Rosa Luxemburg Reader*, pp. 281–311. Luxemburg's book was not published until after her death, in 1921, but the criticisms contained in it were widely known at the time (she took pains to ensure that a number of handwritten copies of the manuscript were circulated upon her release from prison in November 1918) and were expressed as well in a number of articles that she did publish.
49. Fanon, *The Wretched of the Earth*, p. 61.
50. Ibid., p. 55.
51. Gilly, "Introduction," in *A Dying Colonialism*, p. 13.
52. Fanon, "This Africa to Come," in *Toward the African Revolution*, p. 186.
53. Quoted in Cherki, *Frantz Fanon: A Portrait*, p. 156.
54. Ibid., pp. 156–7.
55. Fanon, *The Wretched of the Earth*, p. 106.
56. Ibid., pp. 106–7.
57. Ibid., pp. 107–8.
58. Ibid., p. 151.
59. Quoted in Cherki, *Frantz Fanon: A Portrait*, p. 199.
60. Ibid., p. 95.
61. Fanon, "West Indians and Africans," in *Toward the African Revolution*, p. 18.
62. Ibid., p. 142.
63. For more on this, see Peter Hudis, *Marx's Concept of the Alternative to Capitalism* (Chicago: Haymarket, 2013).
64. Fanon, *The Wretched of the Earth*, p. 143.
65. Ibid., p. 229.
66. Ibid., p. 144.

67. Hegel, *Science of Logic* Vol. II, p. 470.

68. Fanon, *The Wretched of the Earth*, p. 219.

69. As Nietzsche wrote, "And if something great has failed you, does it follow that you yourselves are failures? And if you yourselves are failures, does it follow that *man* is a failure? But if man is a failure—well then!" See *Thus Spoke Zarathustra*, in Walter Kaufmann (ed.), *The Portable Nietzsche* (New York: The Viking Press, 1968), p. 404.

70. Fanon, *The Wretched of the Earth*, pp. 237–8.

Index

Index

Index

Index

Index